THE PSYCHOLOGY OF MODERN HIERARCHIES

First edition
March 2021

The Psychology of Modern Hierarchies

John Almeryn

The theories in this book are also included in a larger book titled "A Theory of Everyone", also by John Almeryn, which explores more aspects of our modern lives.

Contents

1

Introduction

Modern hierarchies can be very complex. In the modern world, there are so many competing factors, mis-matches, and varied difficulties. It means that social hierarchies are no longer a simple pecking order.

Ever since humanity started living in civilisations, with large societies and varied social lives, things have been different. In civilisations, it is no longer the case that a group of people has a well-established hierarchy, all singing from the same hymn sheet. It is no longer the case that a group of people are all aligned to the same idea of what the "correct" social order, and an alpha, should look like. Now, in the modern world, each member of a group might feel about it differently, and have a different idea of how it should be organised.

But, once upon a time, there was greater commonality in human social groups.

For the vast majority of our evolution, our hunter-gatherer ancestors lived in small tribes. In these tribes, the social order would be simple, and everyone would be committed to a group structure that was well cemented and didn't change over time. We would generally only be part of one group, and we would stay with that group our whole lives. The group would be based around survival, and the pecking order would be quite fixed, mutually acceptable, and a hunter-gatherer alpha was probably easy to spot.

However, humanity moved on from our hunter-gatherer past.

We started to live in small farmsteads and villages, and then vast cities and civilisations, driven by economies and different professions. Our social groups became more complicated, our social lives larger, and there was much greater variety within each individual group. Now the alphas took a majority of forms, and, depending on the circumstances, and the surrounding social environment, the same group of people could (potentially) be arranged in a number of different ways.

For example, depending upon the prevailing sub-culture of a particular group, a person can be positioned high or low. In one group, our face might fit, or we may reach a role of persona through good fortune. But in another, we may struggle to attain a similar social position.

This makes our social lives more complex, with greater and more varied competition. It is the "norm" in the modern world, but it is nevertheless different to the environment that we evolved in, where our psychology was formed.

However, this can lead to certain complications, for example to an individual. A person needs groups in order to fulfil our programming, but when those groups are more complicated, it can affect our feelings of identity. This, in turn, then affects the hierarchies themselves.

Therefore to understand modern hierarchies, we have to understand the modern individual.

For example, an individual needs a firm idea of who they are. But this is now harder to find. And, given we have social lives spread over several groups, there may be the odd inconsistency or two. For example, there may be some things about us that we can't change, but that don't fit with who we feel we are. This comes from the idea that we have some things about us that are fixed, that are very difficult to change, but some things that are more flexible, and that can mould themselves into different shapes, based on the people around us.

This makes a concrete identity more difficult to form. And everyone is facing this quandary. In a group, each person will be trying to find a balance between competing forces in their mind, for example between who they need to be, how they come across, and how they respond to the world around them.

We still need an identity and self-belief, but now there can be parts of our personality that aren't completely consistent with what our identity is.

With regard to modern hierarchies, this can then have consequences. For example people can have certain personas (or positions) in a group, despite the fact that a small part of their brain is expecting them to fulfil a different social role. This happens a lot and is fairly normal, but it means that hierarchies are full of people that are perhaps in a slightly different position to the one that their fixed nature might be expecting, and there can be some fallout from this, as a result.

This book explores these two ideas.

It briefly examines how the nature of hierarchical competition has changed throughout humanities history, and then it looks at how an individual fits into a modern hierarchy, and how the hierarchy is then influenced by each person's competing needs.

This is all brought together in Chapter 4, where a modern group is discussed, showing the influence of increased competition, and the influence of modern individuals, who perhaps may not have completely concrete and consistent identities.

However, before that, we can consider a brief history of our journey from hunter-gatherers to where we are today in the modern world.

A (very) brief history of us

Firstly, we have to understand where we've come from, in order to place modern hierarchies in context.

To reach where we are today, to be a modern human, has been less of a gradual change, and more of a roller-coaster ride, catapulting us forward. The following few sections give a brief description of how being a human has changed over time.

1859

Before starting at the beginning, we can briefly consider 1859. This was a year that our understanding of our early history took a large step forwards: when Charles Darwin published *On the Origin of Species*.

The book was met with scepticism and opposition, but nevertheless sold out quickly on its first publishing run[1].

Darwin had written the book after travelling the world on the wooden ship HMS Beagle. A 22-year-old Darwin set sail as a passenger on the ship in 1831, leaving behind the crowded streets foggy London. The world was a changing place, and that was no more so than in England. The fog in Victorian London was air pollution from the first industrial revolution, that was in full swing at the time. Humans had learnt how to harness the energy from burning coal (which has greater energy density, and burns hotter than wood), and to use that energy to turn machines, that were engineered for mass manufacture.

The HMS Beagle crossed the Atlantic and spent a large amount of its voyage around South America. As a botanist, Darwin was cataloguing the flora and fauna he observed. He did this by hand, through beautiful sketches of the plants and wildlife around him (since there was no practical means of photography in the early 1800s).

Around the Galapagos islands, Darwin noticed differences in animals from one island to the next. Animals of similar species, separated by stretches of water, had noticeably different characteristics. He started to form the theory of evolution. He theorised that animals slowly adapt to their environment, and that animals separated on different islands were adapting in different ways. Over time, these adaptations led to large scale changes in a species.

Turning these theories on ourselves, Darwin theorised that humans evolved from apes. He wrote *On the Origin of Species*, and, when it was published in 1859, the wider world considered evolution for the first time.

We now largely believe this is true, and much evidence has been found, in fossils, that show our evolutionary journey. We understand that humans diverged from chimpanzees, around 4-6 million years ago, and became bipedal (stood up) for the first time.

2 million BC

Many, many species of humans used to exist. As we evolved over millions of years, various adaptions caused changes in how certain humans looked and behaved compared to others. At one point, there would have been many different species of human living side by side. Nevertheless, nature had its way, and the more successful species survived and expanded, and the others disappeared.

About 2 million years ago, Homo Erectus emerged. Homo Erectus was our predecessor, and of roughly similar size to ourselves. Roughly speaking, we can consider Homo Erectus as our "parent" species. From Homo Erectus, two "child" species evolved: Homo Sapiens (that's us), and Homo Neanderthalis (Neanderthals)[2].

Homo Erectus was the trailblazer. They started to develop more complex tools, and, significantly, they mastered fire, and used it for cooking.

The mastery of fire was an instigator for change. Cooked food is better in a number of ways. Cooking breaks down tough plant fibres and cell walls, meaning it takes less energy to chew. Cooking also breaks down the various proteins, carbohydrates and sugars, making them easier to digest. When we digest cooked food, we absorb more nutrition from it, compared to uncooked food[3].

This is why cooking smells good to us, and why cooking releases new, enjoyable flavours. Cooked food is more energy efficient, and our brains are still thinking like hunter-gatherers, subtly urging us towards more "advantageous" behaviours.

Cooking resulted in Homo Erectus having more energy available. That allowed their brains to expand (since brain activity is energy intensive). Then, they both had more energy, and greater intelligence. That greater intelligence allowed them to develop new tools, and use more complex language.

Cooking and brain size worked hand-in-hand to elevate our ancestors from just another species on planet Earth, to a highly intelligent and successful one. The path had been set.

200,000 BC

Homo Sapiens didn't arrive on the scene until relatively recently, about 200,000 years ago. Our brains were even bigger than Homo Erectus. With this increased intelligence came greater curiosity, improved use of tools, and we became so good at hunting that we could wipe out entire species around us. As a result, we were more prone to moving around, whether through inquisitiveness, or the desire, or need, for new hunting grounds.

Homo Sapiens migrated out of Africa about 100,000 years ago, and once we got a taste for exploration, we spread out over the entire globe. We got to Australia 50,000 years ago, the pacific islands 33,000 years ago and America 15,000 years ago. Our movements around the world were aided by land bridges no longer there. They were also aided by ice bridges. For much of this time the world was under the grip of an ice age, and the arctic extended as far south as northern Europe[2].

There is evidence to show that the world at the time was full of strange and giant beasts, and that the arrival of Homo Sapiens in an area generally coincided with their disappearance.

Our movements may seem fast, but it was actually fairly slow and gradual. We moved around more than Homo Erectus, or Neanderthals, but only a *little* bit more than them. For example you could walk from North Africa to Australia in about a year, assuming land bridges connected them[4]. So the fact it took Homo Sapiens 50,000 years represents a slow transition, with many generations making no inroads into exploration. However, it appears that our temperament was more biased towards exploring than some of our nearest kin, who were more static.

At one point, for many thousands of years, Homo Sapiens (us) lived alongside our "sibling" species, Neanderthals, in Europe, and alongside our "parent" species, Homo Erectus, in Asia. However, around 25-50,000 years ago, both Neanderthals and Homo Erectus became extinct, leaving just ourselves.

It is not conclusively known how and why Homo Sapiens became the only surviving species of human. Perhaps we have a dark secret, and we were responsible for their extinction. However, there is evidence of peace and interbreeding amongst species, so it could be just circumstance, survivability, or the fact that we were spread further (so that if disaster occurred in one place, we'd survive in another).

10,000 BC

10,000 BC was when it all changed. Before that, for millions of years, the various species of human, Homo Sapiens included, lived in a very similar way: as hunter-gatherers. We would move around the ancient landscapes, picking fruit and berries, and hunting the local wildlife. We would set camp for the night, and spend the evening around a fire, cooking and telling stories, with our close tribe of friends and family.

Around 10,000 BC, in several different locations on Earth, for example Mesopotamia (modern day Syria) and China, we started farming. We settled down to one particular spot, and cultivated a plot of land for a particular crop. People gravitated towards this new technology. Those in these settlements had greater power and security, compared to the wandering hunter-gatherers. Soon, to not be a part of this changing world left small tribes vulnerable, and technologically inferior.

This was the stone age. We gave up our freedom and ability to roam, and instead lived in houses made of stone and mud. We became farmers, and worked together to grow crops and irrigate farmland: digging and maintaining the ditches and waterways.

With greater co-location, humans got their first taste of small society, with all its benefits and compromises.

Nevertheless, by all accounts this was a peaceful period for human beings. The towns and villages were small, bountiful, and remote, so there wasn't motivation for war, or group conflict. Life was also fairly straightforward, as people had relatively few possessions, and the ability to build their own houses, and therefore an element of self-determination (although less so than in the hunter-gatherer lifestyle we'd given up). The year revolved around the harvests, the warmth of summer, and the harshness of winter. Things stayed roughly similar for 7000 years, so there was stability and security. It was a period of co-operation, and learning to live together.

However, the population was slowly growing. Between 10,000 BC and 3,000 BC the population of humans on Earth grew many times, and small villages became towns, and then bigger still[5].

3000 BC

Around 3,000 BC, civilisations started to appear, and the bronze age began.

Vast collections of humans banded together, under single rule, and shared belief. They were based around the main rivers of the world, for example the Nile in Egypt, the Euphrates (and Tigris) in Mesopotamia, the Yellow River in China, and the Indus in India. The world became one of cities and empires, rulers and subordinates. and huge armies regularly went to war over power and resources.

Against all this, humans had lost their self-determination, and were now dependent on others, in the societies they found themselves in.

The ruling class grew in size and power, and started to interlink themselves with the belief systems. Rulers, feeling the power of being in charge of huge numbers of people, now claimed that they were on a par with the gods themselves, and a priestly class emerged, devoted to maintaining and spreading this message.

Mythology therefore became more important. It satisfied the egos of kings and queens, pharaohs and warlords. It reinforced their power, and it united large groups of disparate peoples, under a common culture.

The sky, with its unexplained and unreachable celestial objects, was an obvious basis for these common belief systems. As a result, mythology became intertwined with cosmology.

The priestly classes therefore became astronomers. They mapped the stars, and predicted the movements of the various dots of lights. They tried to explain it all, to the awe, fear, and amazement of the growing populations. Human's focus became less on the natural world around them, with its seasonal plants and wildlife, and instead on the sky above.

How different civilisations interpreted the sky above (the same sky that we look at today), can therefore provide a basis for discussing how being a human changed over the next 5000 years.

Most civilisations in the bronze age tried to explain the universe in similar ways. Nearly all believed that the world was flat, with the sky above, and an underworld below. The sun was an important deity in each culture, and that deity would travel across the sky during the day, and through the underworld at night.

For example, the ancient Egyptians believed that the sun was the god Ra, who was depicted with the head of a falcon. Ra was the creator god, and he travelled across the sky on a solar-boat. At night, he travelled through the underworld (called Duat), and fought the god of chaos: Apophis, a giant serpent, who attempted to stop Ra on his journey. Every morning, when the sun rose, Ra was reborn[6].

The Mesopotamians believed that the sun was the god Utu. Utu had a long beard and long arms, and was the god of justice. He rode across the sky on a chariot, from where he saw everything going on below him. At the end of the day, he passed through a gateway in the West, and into the underworld (called Kur). Whilst in the underworld, he was the arbiter of the dead, until he rose again the next day, through a gateway in the East[7].

The Maya, whose civilisation first started to appear around 2000 BC, in the land-bridge that is modern day Mexico, also had similar beliefs. They believed that the sun was Kinich Ahua. When, at sunset, he disappeared into the ground, to a mellowing of light, and a reddening of the sky, it represented the death of the world. During the night, whilst Kinich Ahua was below them, beneath the deepest caves and sinkholes, he transformed into the Night Jaguar, for the long, arduous journey through the underworld. When he rose the next day, and light filled the sky once more, the world was reborn[8].

Each civilisation was trying to make sense of the strange objects in the sky, whilst also creating myths and stories that allowed people to unite. The moon, stars, and constellations all became a source of greater interest.

One dot of light: Venus, was particularly important to early civilisations. Given Venus' proximity to the sun (compared to Earth), we rarely get the chance to see it with the naked eye. It stays close to the sun in the sky, which means that most of the time it is either being drowned out by the light of the sun, or having followed the sun into the night. It is only visible every 9 months or so, when it is furthest from the sun, and only at either sunrise or sunset (as the Morning Star or Evening Star), when the brightness of the nearby sun isn't obscuring it[9].

Due to its infrequent, but regular, appearances, many early civilisations gave Venus special attention. Perhaps it elevated the status of priests who could accurately predict its arrival every 9 months. Perhaps it's infrequent arrivals could be used to signify special messages, depending on the whims of the leaders. Or, given it appears on a cycle of 9 months, which coincides with the length of a human pregnancy, perhaps they simply believed that it was delivering important messages of fertility, and was interlinked with human existence.

To the Mesopotamians, Venus was Inanna, who had a dual role as both the goddess of love and war, and therefore presided over both birth and death[10]. She became one of their most important gods. To the Egyptians Venus was two gods: Tioumoutiri and Ouait (most civilisations at the time didn't realise that the Morning Star and Evening Star were the same object). To the Maya, the Morning Star was Quetzalcoatl, a feathered snake, and a representation of the fertility of the earth, and the Evening Star was Tlaloc, who was depicted as humanoid, with fangs and a feathered headdress, and who was the god of rain.

People would watch for the arrival of Venus, who appeared only briefly every 9 months, at either sunrise or sunset. Venus' arrival would be a significant event, felt across entire civilisations (and the world).

Whilst the tiny dots of light in the sky (that we now know are stars and planets) moved with predictable precision, the humans of that era were still very much unaware of what the celestial bodies were, and truly believed them to be powerful deities.

Because of this, when an unexpected astronomical event occurred, such as an eclipse, it was met with fear and suspicion.

It was interpreted as if it was a direct intervention from the gods. In each civilisation, the sun was seen as a bringer of life, and in a perpetual fight against the forces of death and destruction, who it battled through each night in the underworld, in order to be reborn at sunrise. There was no other logical reason why the sun disappeared each day. Most civilisations saw an eclipse as a fight between the sun and another mythical being, and if the sun lost, it would bring about the end of the world. As a result, when an eclipse happened, most civilisations banged drums, and performed ceremonies and ritual sacrifices, in order to aid their sun-god in its battle[11].

To live during the bronze age would have been a time of superstition and deeply held beliefs. Societies were fragile and experimental, and there was no historical precedent for how to run a civilisation, with its complex balance of law, economy, culture, defence, and personal rights. Many civilisations rose quickly, and fell just as fast.

It was a time of rapid change, and a time of mythology, against a world full of unknowns.

500 BC

Civilisation spread to other corners of the world, and as technology, knowledge, writing, and record keeping advanced, the myths and legends describing the sky above slowly started to contain greater understanding.

For example, around 500 BC, in the people in the Mediterranean, advances in our understanding of the sky started to occur.

These changes happened in iron-age Ancient Greece, with its city states of Athens and Sparta.

On May 28, 585 BC, an eclipse stopped a six-year war between the Medes and Lydians, fought in modern day Turkey. When the sun was covered, it was seen as an omen.

The bloodshed was halted, weapons were put down, and both sides were reportedly anxious for a peace to be agreed, as willed by the gods[12].

Yet, 150 years later, Pericles showed his Greek Army that the eclipse was nothing more than a covering of the sun, by something bigger than his cloak[13].

This change in perception, of an event such as an eclipse, was aided by scientific advancement made at the time. Pythagoras was at the forefront of these.

Pythagoras was the first to propose that the Earth was spherical. By observing the phases of the moon (i.e. the different crescent shapes it makes at different times in the lunar cycle), he deduced that the moon must be spherical. From this, he reasoned that the Earth was spherical too[14].

Ancient Greece was a hot bed of philosophers, and, with each theory and argument, the world around us slowly started to unravel. For example, Aristotle, around 150 years later, added weight to the arguments (that the Earth was spherical) by inferring it from how different constellations are visible at different times throughout the year. Roughly 100 years after that, Greek astronomers calculated the circumference of the Earth.

The sun, the planets, and the stars all moved in intelligible, endless circular paths, but were becoming more explainable, and less of a source of myth and legend.

Nevertheless, astrology played a part in decision making for centuries to come. The celestial objects couldn't quite shed their mythological status, and many leaders throughout history would consult a fortune teller for a horoscope, when in need of advice and guidance.

1600s

In the 2000 years after Pythagoras, the world was a different place, but many aspects of it hadn't changed. Civilisations were still vying for power, led by rulers who saw themselves as vessels for the gods, and wars were commonplace. Democracy was a flower struggling to take root, occasionally growing in places, only to be washed away by tides of inequality.

It wasn't until the 1600s when larger changes started to occur. The first glimpses of a global economy were starting to take shape, and economic empires developed, such as the Dutch East India Company. Democracy was finding firmer ground, for example following the English Civil War. Science was also seeing many advances, and the 1600s can count Galileo, Kepler, Descartes, Fermat, Pascal, Hooke and Isaac Newton among its notable alumni.

Up until the 1600s, our understanding of the stars hadn't changed that much, because until then we could only see them with the naked eye. It wasn't until the invention of the telescope that this changed. The first recorded telescope was by Hans Lipperhey, a Dutch spectacle maker, who filed a patent to one in 1608[15]. The invention of the telescope was game changing in understanding our place in the universe.

Galileo took that invention and turned it to the stars[16]. Looking through a telescope gave a much deeper understanding of the bodies above us, whether the craters on the moon, sunspots and solar flares, the rings of Saturn, or the moons of Jupiter.

Using the telescope allowed Galileo to confirm the phases of Venus (i.e. that Venus, like our moon, appears as a crescent, depending on the locations of Venus, the Earth, and the Sun – this can't be seen with the naked eye). This allowed Galileo to deduce that Venus was spherical, and gave some insight into the relative positions of Venus, the Earth, and the Sun. From this, and other observations, Galileo was able to prove Copernicus' theory that the *sun* was at the centre of the galaxy.

Copernicus' theory of heliocentrism, that the *sun* was at the centre of the galaxy, was one of many competing theories at the time. Previous to Galileo (and therefore without the ability to prove any theory one way or another), they had been debated using philosophical arguments, loosely based on logic.

The Roman Catholic Church was paying attention to these debates. The idea that the *Earth* was the centre of the galaxy, that had been around for 2000 years (since Ancient Greece), had to some extent worked its way into Christian beliefs. Proposing alternative theories was making the Church nervous. In the early days of Galileo's work, it was merely nerves. For example Galileo was allowed to defend himself at a debate in Rome, and Pope Urban VIII personally urged Galileo to pursue arguments both for *and* against heliocentrism. However, as Galileo pursued heliocentrism further, and proved it more completely, the nervousness of the Church caused them to try him, and he was forced to recant his views. Galileo was placed under house arrest, for most of the remainder of his life, in his villa at Arcetri in Florence.

However, his work on astronomy lived on. The weight of scientific evidence, that advanced our understanding of the stars above, and our place in the galaxy, was too much to ignore.

1859

The 1700s and 1800s saw a wealth of enlightened thinking, with philosophers dreaming of better ways of living, and societies based on monarchism and the elite being dismantled around the globe in favour of power for the people. However, it was also a brutal time, with new weapons of war, and nations vying for power against deep rivalries. The development of the world was also sporadic, which resulted in great conflicts of inequality.

Regardless of the world around us, the individual, average human's perception of it had changed. To be a human in the 1800s was to understand much more about the world. By 1859, the same year Darwin published *On the Origin of Species*, we saw a new breed of knowledgeable human. We had gone from hunter-gatherers wandering the landscape, to bronze age man, who banged drums at eclipses, to the educated few arguing about the philosophical nature of the world around us, to a race of human beings who were comparatively well educated, who understood where they came from as a species, and their position in the galaxy.

When, in 1859, a huge astronomical event occurred, people saw it with wonder, not fear. They saw it with joy, not confusion, and as circumstance, not the will of the gods.

In 1859 a huge solar flare hit the Earth's magnetosphere, and caused the largest geomagnetic storm on record. Auroras could be seen across the globe, even near the equator. The storm caused havoc with the telegraph systems of the time. If a similar storm hit Earth today, as nearly happened in 2012, it would cause widespread malfunctioning and damage of electrical equipment, power grids, and satellites[17].

To have the sky filled with strange moving lights, of different colours, is an awe-inspiring event to perceive. Yet the humans of 1859 were mostly educated enough to understand what was happening.

An Australian gold miner, C.F. Herbert, describes the event[18]:

"I was gold-digging at Rokewood, about four miles from Rokewood township (Victoria). Myself and two mates looking out of the tent saw a great reflection in the southern heavens at about 7 o'clock p.m., and in about half an hour, a scene of almost unspeakable beauty presented itself, lights of every imaginable color were issuing from the southern heavens, one color fading away only to give place to another if possible more beautiful than the last ... It was a sight never to be forgotten, and was considered at the time to be the greatest aurora recorded".

This gold miner's understanding of the event, and their emotional reaction: awe rather than fear, is in stark contrast to their ancestors a few thousand years before. It is an impressive feat for any being of planet Earth, to see such a dramatic and unusual change to the sky above them, caused by an eruption of plasma, from a sun 150 million kilometres away, and to understand it, and enjoy it as a spectacle. Humans had come a long way from their past, and lived in a very different world, in a different social environment, and with new perspectives and understandings.

2

Evolving Hierarchies

With our history described, we can now briefly consider how social groups have changed over time, as humans developed into the modern era. This can give us an insight into the nature of the social hierarchies around us, and why there is so much variation in sub-culture from one group to another.

Groups are so important to us as a species. Groups give us laughter, togetherness and belonging. They give us definition, shared joy and purpose.

But, they also contain an element of posturing, positioning and competition. This competition can be stressful, but is necessary for establishing a hierarchy and positions, for allowing the group to co-operate, and have a rough pecking order for mates.

Hunter-gatherers had only one group, and their position in the group was determined in only one way.

That way was likely similar to most group hierarchies across the natural world. The leader of the group is generally the alpha male or female, and generally a natural leader, and perhaps the largest or strongest. This is because nature is harsh and physical, and our early ancestors would have to fight predators, prey and occasionally rival tribes. As a result, within the tribe, challenges happen through an exchange of behaviours, normally involving posturing or physicality. The animal that wins that exchange has the higher social position.

It's likely that as we roamed the landscape as hunter-gatherers, the leader was probably the one that could win a fight, even if most of the time the tribe was harmonious, and relied on the various skills of each member.

As we started to shed our hunter-gatherer lifestyle, and instead live in fixed-location larger communities, we started to get specialisms. We didn't have to know general hunting and survival skills, but instead could now just focus on woodworking or farming. Someone else would deal with defence, tailoring or tool making. Then, in these small societies, humans find that they form social groups with people all of the same specialism. Hierarchies can then form on the basis of how good we were at that particular skill. As societies became more civilised, with laws and punishments, fighting became less acceptable. Even the largest of humans would have to respect and accede to the master crafter in our town, who had plied their trade over a lifetime (even if their brains were still factoring in an element of physical posturing). That master crafter had the knowledge to pass on to them, so they could become a good craftsperson themselves, and contribute to the complex machine of large group living.

As money became more prevalent, groups could be formed on the basis of who had more money, or success. Those with more money can be perceived to be more attractive, and could attain a higher social level within a group, compared to someone bigger and stronger than them. These hierarchies were formed on value, rather than behavioural posturing.

As societies become bigger still, and more structured, we started to have defined roles. Now, hierarchies can be determined simple by who holds that role. For a team of accountants in the pharaoh's treasury department, there is a team leader. The team leader may not be the one who could win a fight, nor be the best at their profession. Instead, they might just have been in the right place at the right time, or been there the longest. Nevertheless, because they hold the position, the others must do what the team leader says, else they won't get the pay rise they need.

All of these forms of establishing hierarchies, whether more behavioural, value or role based, exist to greater or lesser extent in different groups in our present-day environment. They are all necessary for creating stable and peaceful large societies.

However, this creates complexity in our social lives, because as modern humans we have links to more than just one group, and in each group our position is determined according to a different set of criteria. Perhaps among friends it is more down to behaviours. Perhaps at our sports club it could be down to money or prowess at the particular sport. At work it is down to who holds the appropriate roles or positions.

We can therefore find ourselves competing on one criterion one day, and a different criterion the next. At times we can feel that we have instincts that we should be positioned one way, but the prevailing social dynamic in a group positions us differently. We have to keep many plates spinning, which we often do fairly naturally, but which can lead to occasional stress or frustration.

The competition in a group is a bit like playing a board game. Hunter-gatherers would all be competing to the same set of rules, within a well-defined tribe. In contrast, as modern humans, we have greater diversity of competition. In each group, we subtly compete, or argue, that the social rules should be this or that, depending on what gives us the most advantage. We compete over what we're competing on. This can lead to greater stress and frustration, and occasionally the board is knocked into the air, and all the pieces scattered.

Our programming wants to find something resembling a tribe, and to have a varied social life. But, it finds a mix of groups, spread out, and with greater, more unusual conflicts within them. This can add difficulty to our lives, in the same way it did for our ancestors in civilisations, several thousand years ago.

Large societies add greater social complexity, to the groups that we need to fulfil our programming.

3

Inherited Hierarchies

But it is not just more varied competition that characterises modern hierarchies. We also have to consider how an individual fits into a group. Modern groups are full of people who are each approaching the same thing from a contrasting angle. And when our modern lives are more complex, there can then be mis-matches and unusual conflicts.

This can create dilemmas for an individual, which in turn affects the hierarchies themselves.

Therefore, in order to understand modern hierarchies, we have to understand the modern individual. Hierarchies are made up on individuals, each turning over quandaries in their minds, and trying to make loose ends in their lives fit. A modern hierarchy is made up of a group of people who perhaps are all thinking differently, are affected by other, different social groups, and who have come from different circumstances.

This chapter considers the individual, in order to give us a basis for exploring the interactions between individuals in the next chapter.

So, in order to start unravelling what is going on for an individual in a modern hierarchy, we can begin by considering some questions.

In a tribe of hunter-gatherers, if each member wants to maximise their value, why aren't they always trying to get to the head of the tribe? Why isn't there constant fighting, with those at the top having to defend themselves against all-comers, all the time?

You can envisage a scenario where, after waking up each morning, there is a series of conflicts to arrange the hierarchy for that day. How can the tribe move together, with individuals trying to get the best for themselves?

In reality, to oppose the force of each hunter-gatherer wanting to maximise their own value, I propose the idea that there is a stabilising force: their inherited position.

The inherited position is relatively fixed throughout each tribesperson's lifetimes. Whilst rearranging can (and often does) happen, and each tribes-member has an identity that is theirs, they also have a more fixed nature. We are after all, part fixed, part flexible. With regard to hierarchies, part of that fixed nature is represented in our inherited position.

The inherited position creates a bias that makes it harder to rearrange the tribe. As a result, less energy is spent on infighting. This leaves more energy for the important survival tasks of hunting, defending themselves from predators, foraging, building shelters, and keeping themselves warm.

Whilst these biases make it harder to rearrange the tribe, it can, and often needs to be done. It's just a little harder, and requires overcoming how those biases make the tribespeople feel. The inherited position is merely an anchor, and there is flexibility to allow positions to be arranged according to the specific environment. We are after all, part fixed, part flexible.

We see this ability to rearrange social groups across the animal kingdom. For example, when a leader becomes too aggressive, or less moral and fair, or isn't supported by the group anymore, then the group tends to overthrow them. However, it takes a certain upswell or force for this to happen.

To illustrate this in humans, we can consider a tribe of ancient hunter-gatherers travelling north through Arabia, in search of new animals to hunt. They had passed a different tribe a few months ago, who had told them of better hunting in the north, as they had exchanged news and stories.

The leader of our tribe, who has always been good and fair, is getting older, and is less good at leading long-distance travel. Another, more youthful member, had always dealt with tracking and direction. As they set out on their journey, arguments ensue about whether they should head for the mountains or the plains. The more youthful tribesperson feels strongly about the plains, and feels that the leader is being too cautious. They gain some support amongst the tribe, and eventually decide to usurp the leader. It takes some courage. When they decide to take action, they feel something pressing against them, something in their brain says don't do it. They feel an invisible force that they must overcome. However, the younger tribesperson has strong will, and manages to override those feelings, and, after challenging the old leader, they are successful at establishing themselves as the new one. It feels good, and they feel an immediate elevation in their status.

Yet, they wake up the next morning, and the previous leader is still there. They look at the old leader, who had been in charge of the tribe for their whole life, and something in their brain finds it hard to recognise the new arrangement, with them in command. Those feelings, that they had to overcome

31

to usurp the leader, are still there. They feel number one: they earnt it, and deserve it; but a part of them, frustratingly and confusingly, is still responding as if they're number two. Because of this, they have to be a little harsher to the previous leader, to ensure that they maintain the new arrangement, and be a leader over someone who they had looked up to their whole lives.

The new leader is feeling two things at once. They are feeling some effects of their lifelong position as number two, but also a firm belief, or need, to be number one. The difference between the two is affecting their behaviour.

In the modern world these inherited positions are still there. We all have them, biases that channel and restrain us towards certain positions. They are the part of us that is fixed. They ensure some stability to our groups, whether a small friendship group, or a large society, by ensuring there is some resistance to constant rearranging.

We also have the part of us that is flexible, that can adapt to our circumstances, and it allows us to move around in society, and develop and identity that is ours. Against that identity, the inherited position mostly becomes an unwelcome inconvenience, that often simply makes it harder to be our identity, or to strive for an identity we want. We have an anchor that doesn't move, but we are only loosely connected to it by a stretchy rope, so that we can move around as our circumstances require.

Our inherited position is part of us, and our brain reacts to our environment based on it. We mostly don't notice it, and it is something that happens in the background. It shapes our lives and behaviours, but it only occasionally rears its head in our day to day lives, for example when our behaviours become harder to do. The inherited position is representative of our fixed nature, and is passed down family lines in a cascade.

In the modern world, it's easier to understand when we consider large distances between the positions of people in society. For example, when your average person meets a leader or celebrity, we often feel some of those subconscious effects, that our position creates. Our brain is recognising the difference in position, and we're reacting to that leader or celebrity accordingly. People often find they are nervous, find it harder to speak, or don't know what to say. These are all resisting forces, and are the same forces that our number two had to overcome to become the new tribe leader.

In our social and professional lives, those forces are at play, but on a much smaller scale. We have two things, how we emotionally respond to situations, which is determined by our inherited position, and who we feel we need to be, or are: our identity. The first is more fixed, the second is more flexible. Our behaviours, that we've learnt throughout our lives, will account for any different between the two.

Positions in a tribe are relatively simple. There will be a fairly linear pecking order, which may have small variations depending on what activity the tribe is doing, but nevertheless they will be fairly fixed. When we consider our large societies, where there are effectively thousands or millions of small tribes all interlinked, it can get quite complicated. For example, there will be leaders in groups at the top of society, but also leaders in groups at the bottom.

There are effectively two main ways large societies are arranged. One is our overall position in society, and the other is our social role in the groups we are a part of. We see and react to people in a "societal status" way, as well as an "interpersonal way".

The first is more related to our level or perceived value in that large societal hierarchy, whilst the second is more related to social skills, and perceptions of the type of personalities or attributes that we react to as above and below us.

This leads to two strands of our inherited position: a value one, and a social one.

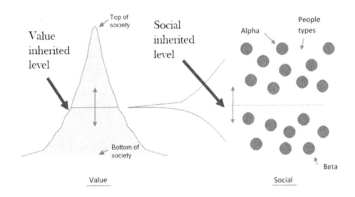

Our *value* inherited position determines who our brain reacts to, without our conscious input, as above and below us in society.

Our *social* inherited position determines who our brain reacts to, without our conscious input, as above and below us in our interpersonal interactions, i.e. the type of people we accede to, and the type of people we don't (in an isolated tribe, we'd only have a "social inherited level", and not a "value inherited level").

The inherited positions are not who the parent thinks they are: that is their identity. As we shall come onto in a scenario (later in this chapter), the inherited positions are merely a slowly changing position, from one generation to the next.

Hierarchies, and the pecking order, play an important part in nature. Because they are important, so they must have an effect on us. We have parts of us that are fixed, and parts of us that are flexible. Considering hierarchies, the part that is fixed is our inherited positions (value and social). These can be difficult to change throughout our lives.

They're relatively fixed because they're a stabilising force. They're the force trying to prevent hierarchies rearranging too quickly, and becoming erratic, with too much energy spent on infighting. They slow down changes in groups (whether a tribe or society), perhaps to a generational pace, so that any changes that do happen can be absorbed and approved of. Therefore, we can change where we are in hierarchies, and our identity can be anything that we can feel supported in, but the further it is from our anchor, perhaps the harder it is to maintain.

Whilst the inherited position exists, and we might notice it in others, we don't really want to believe it in ourselves. To us, there is only one position, our identity. We *are* our identity. That defines us. The fact that we occasionally react, and feel, inconsistent with that identity is more confusion and frustration, rather than recognition of a second level.

If our inherited position is our fixed part, then our identity is our flexible part. After all, in the modern world, people say you can be anything. They say dream big, become a star, emulate your role model. And to some extent this is possible. Whatever our starting point in life, it's at least theoretically possible to move to another, and believe we are that new level. It generally requires one thing – acceptance within the group at the new level. We can't simply decide where we want to go and be there. We may not fully feel it, until we are welcomed, and treated with acceptance, at that level, by the people there.

This acceptance at the higher level, even for a short time, has a powerful effect on us. Our identity can change very quickly from this, and we then believe that's who we are. We judge others in the same way that people of our new level judge others. We associate and believe we're similar to the people around us at the new level. The new level becomes our identity level. Our group driver, to be interlinked and a reflection of the group we associate with, provides us with new self-belief.

We therefore have two levels. We have our inherited position; and our identity, and they can often be different. This forms the basis of the theories proposed in this book.

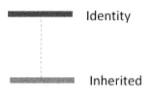

Our identity is **who we believe we are**, who we associate with, perhaps our achievements, our job, and our role in society.

Our inherited position is subconsciously where we fit in, and defines **how we emotionally respond** to the people around us.

There can be a difference between the two. Our identity and our inherited position can be at different levels: they can be *diverged.*

When we are diverged, so that our inherited and identity levels are different, everything is a little harder, and difficult to interpret. At times we may be reacting to things one way (based on our inherited level), but needing to feel about them a different way (in order to fulfil our identity level). We need to be our identity level, because it is the level that defines us, the level that we need to be in order to feel association with the group that we feel closest to: the level we feel most ourselves in.

The main way we bridge the gap between the two, to steamroller over our inherited level, and achieve our identity level more often, is through behaviours. Our behaviours can become a little more obtrusive, in order to ensure people treat us more according to our identity, and not our inherited position.

This is a form of human duality, between our fixed parts, that ensure we follow patterns, and flexible parts, that allow us to adapt to our circumstances.

In terms of where the inherited position comes from, then, as the name suggests, we pick it up from our interactions throughout our adolescence, but, mostly, we pick it up from our parents.

Our inherited level is tied to our parents. They are the source of the parts of us that our fixed, since they are one of the only sureties in life. It also comes from them because they are a force, often unfortunately, that is difficult to deviate from. We have many different forces pulling us towards them, and just as sometimes we have to resist our parents, we also have to resist some of the forces coming from our inherited position. Often we can do both, or reach compromises, without too much difficulty, or even noticing, but sometimes it takes a lot of strength.

In order to learn behaviours that are human, we are linked to our parents. We copy behaviours off them, but also emotions. We copy how they respond to people around them, and this replicates itself in us. From this we have an inherited position, as well as behaviours that fit with that position, to allow us to seamlessly fit into social groups we come across, at least theoretically.

The son our daughter of the tribe leader will grow up simply feeling less inhibited taking leadership positions, and feel less of a barrier to taking command of situations. They will learn leadership behaviours from their parent to go with their position as they grow.

The son or daughter of a number two in a tribe, will do similar, with respect to number two. They may feel some barrier to taking the lead, preferring instead to support the number one. Perhaps they test the number one from time to time, as they grow up together, but find that the number one simply has a small advantage, in that the conflict is less of a threat, and easier to dismiss or win.

Our *inherited level* is representative of our anchor to our **parents**. Our inherited position largely comes from our parents. We pick up on how they emotionally respond to different people, and that replicates itself in how we do, without us consciously affecting it.

On the other hand, our *identity level* is representative of our driver to define ourselves in relation to the **group** of people around us, as well as being influenced by our driver to **maximise our value**.

The *inherited level* is more fixed. It is very difficult to change, even throughout our lifetime. It is a stake in the sand after all, and part of the more fundamental tie to our parents to ensure our behaviours don't stray too far from theirs. It gets ingrained in all our relationships, and linked to our starting point in life.

The *identity level* is more flexible. Providing we achieve acceptance; it can basically be at any level. It can jump to the new level very quickly. It tends to only go up. We always hold on to that highest position, even if we are only keeping it in our back pocket.

Because the identity level and inherited level are driven by such fundamental forces, they can have a large impact on how we behave and how we feel, in ourselves, and towards others. They can be a cause of difficulty, especially if they're different, and we're diverged.

There are two main ways we can be diverged: in value; and in social skills:

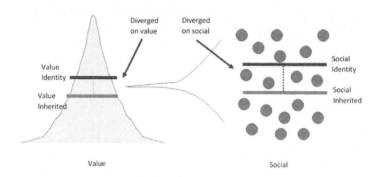

Nevertheless, it gets complicated to consider both at the same time, and often the effect of levels on interpersonal interactions is coming from differences in either value or social skills. In reality, our inherited position is a map that is different in different environments, whereas our identity is normally more singular.

We can avoid this complexity however, because in most cases, and most environments, there is only one inherited level that is important, and one identity level. The complexity reduces to those two: how we respond to a situation, and who we feel we need to be in that situation.

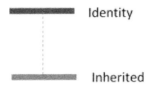

Identity

Inherited

This simplification is all we need to describe most behaviours that we see in people around us. For most people, we can simply consider that they are diverged or not, in a certain situation, or across key portions of their life, and interpret their experiences and behaviours from that.

In large modern societies, everyone is diverged to some extent. In a tribe, our inherited position and identity are merely about the pecking order, but, in large societies, where we interact with many different groups, different sub-cultures, and have our social lives spread over several groups, we add on a little social resistance. As we will come onto, this "social delta", that causes the vast majority of modern humans to be diverged, means that most people have extra reservations about their social interactions, beyond mere positions, and everyone is behaving as if they were trying to attain positions slightly above their inherited position (including the generations before us).

The "social delta" causes everyone to diverge, as we all face greater headwinds in our life than merely hierarchical positions in a tribe.

However, some people are more diverged than others. Some people diverge in value, and find acceptance at a higher place in society. This often happens through success or wealth accumulation, where we can afford to move to a higher status area, or socially climb. Some people diverge in social skills, and attain positions in groups above their inherited position.

This can happen at work, where leaders or managers can attain a leadership role in interactions, which they might not achieve in their purely social interactions outside of that role. Or it can happen when someone has favourable attributes (compared to their ancestors) that allows them to take higher roles in social groups.

But however diverged we are, to us, there is only one level, the identity level. The people around us, at that level, are fulfilling an important part of how a human feels about themselves. We are them, and they are us. We move with them, they are the ones we integrate and copy, and who have our back. This is drawn from a key human driver, to fit into a group and integrate with them, which makes us feel a part of them, so it is a strong force. To be treated as less than that identity level can be quite hurtful. But nevertheless, the two levels are there, and have an impact on behaviours and interactions.

This can be one of the greatest difficulties of being a human living in large societies: the conflict between our inherited level, and the need to associate with the group of people in front of us. We can be pulled in two directions at once, and become more stretched, if those two are different.

Our brain is very good at shaping our views to fit. We can disregard large amounts of what's in front of us in order that we are our identity level regardless of our inherited level. We can dismiss certain interactions, people, or facts about ourselves. We are still hunter-gatherers, and our brain is shaping how we feel about ourselves in hunter-gatherer ways. Our brain wants certainty of who we are, and a firm identity, that it would get so easily in a hunter-gatherer tribe.

If people treat us according to our identity level, all is well. If they don't, there can be conflict. Bringing up what you think someone's inherited level is will serve no purpose, the information here is for our own internal understanding. When conflict arises because of levels, for example someone being overly obtrusive, or people not treating others according to their identity level, or people feeling constrained by their inherited level, then, because our levels are such fundamental forces that are difficult to change, we have to make the conflict about something else. We form beliefs, driven by our levels, that allow us to integrate our personal circumstances into society.

Our inherited position and our identity position form a large part of who we are, but unpicking them is often elusive. Plus, there is often little we can realistically do about them. We can learn to live around them, or change our behaviours to better suit them, but changing them fundamentally is very difficult, seeing as how they are derived from our core drivers, and therefore come from quite a deep place. Nevertheless, they play a large role in how we, and others, see the world and behave, and so to understand this, we have to consider them.

4

A Modern Group

With an understand of each individual, and how each person feels at least some effects of their fixed and flexible natures, we can now explore how this plays out across a group.

In towns and cities throughout history, people have been forming groups with people from different backgrounds, walks of life, and who've had very different experiences.

When a group forms, our social instincts kick in. Our hunter-gatherer brain assesses the goings on in the group with some importance. The dynamic of the group, what it represents, and how we are positioned in the group, can have a big impact on us. Our focus tends to be drawn into the group, and any conflict there, in isolation from the society around us.

Those hunter-gatherer instincts are there to move the group towards a common point, where there is order, harmony, and each person's needs are accounted for. However, when the group is made up of people from different parts of a large, unequal society, this process can be harder than it should be.

For example, each person in the group, because they are from different backgrounds and experiences, will have different preconceptions about how and where they fit into the group. Their backgrounds and experiences will affect how they subconsciously react to the group in front of them, as well as where they feel they need to be positioned.

With regard to "levels", each person in the group will be **diverged** to a greater or lesser extent. For example, one person may identify as a leader, but find they have to do so against a strong headwind of a low inherited position. Another may feel out of place in a group of higher social status.

Each person therefore has their inherited level and their identity level. Much of what goes on in the group is about the interactions between the mix of the various levels.

When a group of modern humans comes together, they tend to be a slightly mismatched melting pot of different respective levels. Below is an example of 8 people who have just been thrown together in a new group.

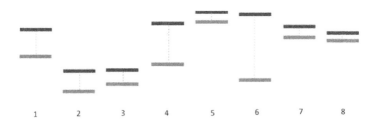

They could be a group of frontiers men and women, banding together to head across the Rocky Mountains, in the early 1800s, in search of wealth, and a better life on the West coast of America. They could be a group heading across the silk road from Chang'an in 700 AD, when Tang dynasty China brought about a golden age of arts and culture. It could have been a group in the aristocracy of Hapsburg Austria, or a group of slaves in the Mesopotamian empire. The levels are relative to each other, so apply to any human, in any part of society.

This coming together of different levels is a melting pot of a situation, but our social instincts deal with it fairly well. We tend to pick up on the other people's inherited and identity levels. People signal who they feel they are, how they want to be treated, compromises are made, and a rough structure starts to form.

There will then be two things going on. One is that the group is naturally pulled together towards a common point, and the other is the fallout (i.e. interpersonal conflict) from the fact that the group can't fully reach a common point. We shall firstly look at how the group is pulled together, before looking at the interpersonal relationships.

Levelling the playing field

On the first point, after the group has been thrown together, it will start to revolve around a single new sub-culture, which will be an amalgamation of the different sub-cultures of the new members. The group finds a level of commonality, and, as the group establishes itself, each member feels acceptance at the group level. Our brains start drawing definition from those around us, copying and interlinking behaviours, so that we become a reflection of those around us, to allow the group to move as one. A group structure forms, with rough positions and alliances, until the group dynamic looks like this:

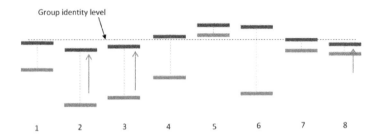

The inherited levels won't have changed, but the identity levels have been affected by the formation of, and acceptance within, the new group.

Particularly for persons 2 and 3, and lesser so for person 8, the acceptance in the new group has raised their identity level. It can happen very quickly, and this group then becomes those person's highest acceptance group, and therefore their new maximum status.

Their identity will quickly form as a reflection of those around them in the new group. They will judge themselves by those around them, seeking comparison, feeling elevated by their acceptance, but also finding new competitions, and perhaps new social pressures too. Looking outwardly from the group, they will now judge others from the viewpoint of the new group, including old friends, and even family.

However, despite the commonality and coalescing of the new group into a single structure, each person is linked to other groups that also influence them, and the group will appear, and mean, different things to each member. The members in the group are also anchored to different points, some far away from the group's identity level.

The external forces are manifested in different levels of divergence on individuals, which result in the members of the group being obtrusive towards each other, and competing and posturing in order to achieve identity levels, in the group, against the totality of their social lives.

As each member is diverged, to a greater or lesser extent, each has to be obtrusive to maintain their identity level against the pull from the elastic to their anchor: their inherited level. Those who are more diverged will be more obtrusive, and so the inherited levels (the anchor points of each person), are feeding into the group dynamic.

The playing field isn't level beforehand, different members of the group are trying to achieve their positions, with differing distances to their anchor point. Some are facing a greater pull towards that anchor point than others.

This isn't always a problem, far from it, it is the norm in the modern world. In fact this obtrusiveness is the levelling mechanism. It is sharing the difficulty of being diverged. It is evening out the difficulty felt by some more than others, and, results in a more even playing field.

The obtrusiveness is also making it harder for those with identities *above* the group identity level to maintain them. They face some of the obtrusiveness of others overcoming their inherited levels, and feel less able to fully project a personality representative of a higher status level. That personality will have come from a different group. If they fully expressed it in the current group, it would be trying to move the group away from the common group identity level; and make it harder for those who are diverged to maintain their own identities in the group.

As a result, in the group, those with the highest identity levels will have them reduced a little. They will still maintain their identity levels, but elsewhere, and find they have to let go of it a little when in this group. Overall, each person in the group has had their identity moved towards a common level.

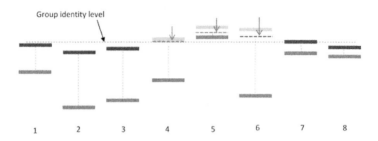

For those that the new group has given a boost to, the group will be quite important to them, as it is the source of their max status, and therefore their identity.

They are also now more diverged, which means greater distance to their subcon, and greater pull towards it, from time to time.

On the other hand, for those reduced a little, the group will mean much less, and they will instead rely more on other groups they are a part of, where they can achieve their identity level more uninhibited.

Our inherited level, and need to be our identity level, are strong forces. They are also relatively fixed by circumstances, so this process of levelling is almost impossible to circumvent. It happens one way or the other, even if people are trying to avoid it, trying not to be obtrusive, or trying not to integrate.

Once it has happened, the group has now formed. The flexible part of people's levels (their *identity* level) has been changed by the formation of the group, whilst the fixed part of people's levels (their *inherited* level) remains the same, and feeds into the resulting group dynamic. We tend not to think of groups in this way, it is a process that simply happens, based off our social instincts, and the emotions they produce. Nevertheless, it can explain much of the interpersonal behaviour we see.

The resulting group dynamic, that persists after the group has formed, will still be unusual conflicts coming from levels, and these can now be briefly looked at. Most conflict comes down to the relative levels of the people involved.

Group interpersonal relationships

Person 5 has the highest identity and subcon, so they are likely the leader of the group. However, person 6 has an identity close to 5, but a much lower subcon. It's likely that at times person 6 thinks they are the leader (or the alpha) of the group, until they are gently overruled by person 5.

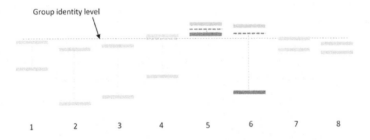

Group identity level

1   2   3   4   5   6   7   8

Person 5 occasionally has to keep person 6 in check, because, if person 6 gets too confident, they tend to be a little disruptive of the group, or treat people in ways they aren't happy with. For example, person 6 may try to lead and support people from the viewpoint of their identity level, but to others, it feels like it is coming from their inherited level. That can feel uncomfortable to the others. The members of the group sense the difference in inherited positions between person 5 and person 6. As humans we pick up on a huge amount of information, and read body language and expressions quite accurately, even on brief first impressions. To be led by someone we don't feel justifies the position can be frustrating.

In order to try to maintain their identity therefore, person 6 will have to be more obtrusive towards the others. They are unlikely to blend into the group seamlessly.

Perhaps person 6 could form an alliance with person 5. However, this would be unlikely to be a two-way, close friendship, and instead be more of an alliance of convenience.

Person 6 may find it difficult to interact with the group when person 5 isn't there, partly due to their obtrusiveness, and partly due to needing the group to treat them according to their diverged identity. Without person 5, the rest of the group may not support person 6's identity as a leader.

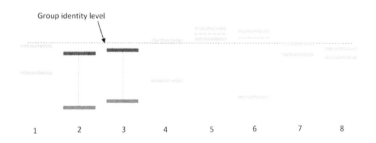

Persons 2 and 3 have the lowest inherited levels. To them, the group represents something that elevates them. They are able to meet the group level and find acceptance, and this is likely through an alliance with each other. As they both have similar inherited levels, they will see the world, and react, in the same way, so they have greater potential for being closer.

They will perhaps be a little cliquey, and be less close to those around them, or, alternatively, they may take on a more supportive role to the other group members. In group situations, it's likely that persons 2 and 3's focus will be more on each other, as friends or competition, and they will pay more attention to what each other is doing than other members of the group.

Persons 2 and 3 can also be peacemakers and leaders in some way. They have quite a secure position in the group, albeit in the lowest position, which allows them to be a stabilising factor. However, perhaps they aren't wholly happy with being in the position they find themselves in, and should unusual circumstances allow, they may wish to raise themselves up a little. We all have that desire, to maximise our value.

Person 7 is in the middle of the group hierarchy through their identity, but the least diverged. They're happy in their position, for example perhaps their parents took similar positions comfortably in similar types of groups, and therefore they don't play too active a role in the group, preferring to stay by the side-lines. Occasionally, someone else in the group tries to challenge them, but because they aren't diverged, they're not too bothered, they can brush it aside more easily, and people leave them to it.

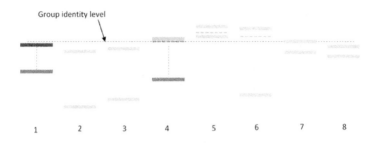

Persons 1 and 4 are the middle of the group, and are somewhat diverged. They sense that they are similar types of people, and, like 2 and 3, perhaps form an alliance, and become quite competitive towards each other. This competitiveness is because both sense the other's inherited levels, but, as is natural for a human being, believe themselves to only have one level, their identity. We tend to see others according to their inherited level, but see ourself according to our identity level. Each will therefore feel themselves above the other. This can cause a "cross-conflict":

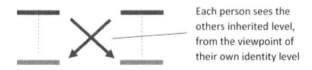

Each person sees the others inherited level, from the viewpoint of their own identity level

This arrangement can escalate relationships somewhat, because it is something that cannot be resolved fundamentally. Both want to establish themselves a little above the other, but neither can (due to their own inherited level), and they can be drawn into conflict or competitiveness as a result. Perhaps this is tolerable or enjoyable at times, in a friendly banter type way. In some ways competing with the other person is a method of maintaining their identity level. Or, perhaps it pushes them apart.

Often, these two people, in such a cross-conflict, will have different values, for example different reasons why they should be positioned above the other. Perhaps these are drawn from other core groups that each of the pair are a part of. For example each person may define themselves according to a different one of the three main types of competition discussed in Chapter 2 (behavioural, value or role based). Neither can recognise the others values, because it would allow the other person to establish themselves above them. Through this type of competition, our own values are reinforced, and harder to stray from.

Therefore, we tend to observe others according to their inherited level, and only treat people according to their identity level when we can, i.e. when it doesn't conflict with us achieving our own identity level. And, whilst we see others according to their inherited level, we see ourself according to our identity level, and struggle to believe that we have an inherited level, that may be apparent to others.

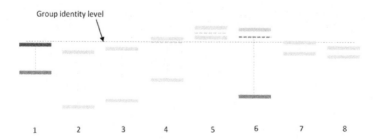

Looking at the friendship that persons 1 and 6 might have, person 6 has both a higher identity and a lower subcon. This arrangement can often produce strange results, and it is unlikely the two are close. Person 6 feels they have a higher identity that person 1, and this has been established in the group sub-culture, but, due to their lower inherited level, they actually feel more out of place in the group from time to time.

Person 6 will be more affected by goings on in the group, and be more emotionally invested in it. Person 6 will be more affected by person 1, than person 1 is by person 6. In conflict between them, person 6 has a higher position, but further to fall.

This can often set up a feedback loop.

This "leveraged-conflict" can result in person 6 being quite controlling. In order to maintain their identity, against a less secure position, they have to be more obtrusive. They have to more greatly rely on the group structure, that enables their higher position, and impress that on person 1. Person 1 senses the lower inherited level of person 6, and so to be talked down on by person 6 is uncomfortable.

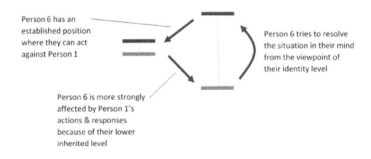

Person 6 has an established position where they can act against Person 1

Person 6 tries to resolve the situation in their mind from the viewpoint of their identity level

Person 6 is more strongly affected by Person 1's actions & responses because of their lower inherited level

In a friendship group, it's likely some distance will be put between persons 1 and 6, in order to minimise tension and conflict. However, there are many examples in life where this type of leveraged social relationship can occur.

One example is when the group has specific roles of responsibility, for example in our profession. If person 6 is a manager (hence the higher identity level), but one of their employees has higher inherited level, the manager may feel insecure in their higher position, and rely on the role, as well as impress the organisational structure on others.

There will be huge variation in how it could play out, depending on the personalities and situation involved, and it may not be a problem at all. If persons 1 and 6 have strong support elsewhere, that maintains their positions, they may not even notice this arrangement.

This group is an example of how our modern social environment, where people are diverged, and with identities forged in different places, can cause conflicts. The differing levels, that are caused by the melting pot of different people coming together to form a group, can collide. Our brains cope with the complexity of the situation, and our social instincts often find compromises and solutions naturally, but levels are hard to cover up completely, and generally greater stress and conflict ensues at times.

For hunter-gatherers, who only had one group, and the group structure and sub-culture was well established, these types of interpersonal conflicts simply didn't happen.

Levelling across society

As an aside, with each group being pulled together towards a common point, this effect occurs across society. In every group, there are social instincts trying to find commonality, and so there is a general trend in society pulling it all together, slowly and methodically over generations, like a tailor stitching a garment together.

We see this when we look throughout history, where power, wealth, rights and freedoms are generally moving in the right direction, towards greater equality.

There are many forces causing this to be so. However, there are also many forces opposing a move to greater equality (otherwise we'd get there in the next few weeks). For example these include: greed; the difficulty in moving around large amounts of wealth and power; the need to hold onto wealth (and be unyielding) vs. the desire to usurp it; the need to compete with contemporaries (with whom we are interlinked with, wherever we are in society); and, not least, the way that an adult human being's perceptions of the world become quite fixed in adulthood (so that they can be a reference point for their growing children, but, as a side effect, they become more resistant to change). Nevertheless, it appears that the forces propelling us towards equality are more powerful than the forces that oppose it.

When the world is a more equal place, where a similar quality of life can be lived wherever we are born, the world will no doubt be a better place to live in. We'd be able to enjoy life as fully as anyone else, and live with a similar quality of life anywhere in the world. We'd be able to enjoy our cultures, respecting similarities and differences to neighbouring ones. We'd be able to compete amongst our social circles with some enjoyment of it, rather than it being stressful, with too much on the line. When/if there is conflict in the world, each person would have less to gain, and less to lose, so can be more amenable, and compromise more easily. We would feel less stretched, and be able to prioritise, and feel, the fulness of family and friendship, which, like our hunter-gatherer ancestors, are some of the most important parts of our life experiences.

We'd give up that feeling of glory and power, but those are short lived, fragile rewards that last only until the next person takes them from us. They are an out of balance driver, that rarely leads to long term fulfilment. And, with a shrinking world, it will become harder and harder to enjoy excess, when we never live too far from those with less. Currently, the top 26 wealthiest people in the world have the same wealth as the bottom 50%: the bottom 3.6 billion people. Perhaps they should all meet up for a conference to debate whether this is a good thing or not.

It's unlikely we'll ever be completely equal, some hierarchy needs to exist for large groups of humans to live side by side, but we can certainly get closer to a more equal, and fairer world. And, whether we want to or not, it appears to be the natural progression.

5

Duality Origins

Now that we've looked at the concept of our fixed part and a flexible part (characterised by our inherited level and our identity level), and how this affects group dynamics and hierarchies, in this last chapter we shall actually go back to looking at an individual again.

The reason for this is that, as proposed (and discussed) in the previous few chapters, the main differentiating factor in modern hierarchies is the idea that people can be diverged. People can have an identity different from how they come across, or different from what their fixed nature is expecting, and this is one of the main complications in modern hierarchies. You can have leaders that have achieved a position they don't appear to be able to back-up, or everyone can be slightly out of position compared to a place in a group they might fit more naturally.

In a group, many or all of the people may be diverged. In order to better understand this concept, we have to look at individuals in more detail, to understand the nature, origins and consequences of divergence. By better understanding the diverged individual (and we are all diverged to some extent), we can then better understand the modern hierarchy.

Therefore, this chapter is considering the modern individual. We shall first look at how a person's *identity level* can change over time, throughout their life, before looking at the *inherited level:* where it comes from, and what its implications are.

Our max identity

Our identity level comes from the highest-level group we've achieved acceptance in.

When we meet new people, we pick up on a lot of information. We may make an initial assessment of them, how they move, and what intentions they might have, and we form a first impression, which is likely to be picking up on their inherited level. Then, often, early on in the conversation, people will drop hints about what their identity level is, and how they want to be treated. It may be a fact about them, an association, such as a group that they are (or were) a part of, or a story of success, present or past. This is their identity level, and is how they see themselves. It is commonly based on their maximum identity achieved.

If we treat them according to their identity level, all is well. Sometimes we can, but sometimes we can't. If we can't, it is normally because their identity is based off a sub-culture that is incompatible with ours, and therefore conflicts with us achieving our own identity level. In this case we have to treat them a little less, which can be a cause of conflict.

The hints that people drop about their identity level are often related to the highest status they've achieved. Our identity only tends to go up. Once we've achieved acceptance at a certain level, it can be very hard to accept ourselves as less than that. This is a representation of our drive to maximise our value. Essentially, if you step back, the human being is attaining a highest level, and then resisting letting go.

If there wasn't a change in ourselves, if we didn't feel more, because of our upwardly jump, then we wouldn't increase in confidence in order to find a mate at this higher level.

The following diagram shows a fictional example of a person's life, with 5 main groups that they've come across. The first friendship group is at school, the second is at college, and then they have three main social groups as an adult. These could be based around work, sport, or social clubs for example.

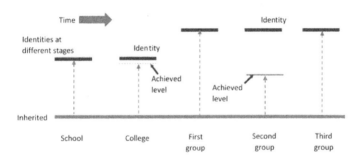

This person's inherited level stays fairly constant throughout their life, but their identity level changes.

Their school has a reasonably high standing compared to their inherited level. This can be fairly normal for modern humans, given how an institution that represents hundreds, and has some history, has more status than an individual.

In this example, the person then goes on to college, but the college doesn't have quite the status of the school. The person has no problem fitting in there, and even feels somewhat at ease, because they have their higher identity level from the school to fall back on. They maintain their identity from the school throughout their time at college.

Then, the first social group they come across after college are people of an even higher social status, perhaps met through a job that the person was fortunate to get, and they fit in there. Their identity level is elevated, and they now feel like the people around them, in that group. They are quite diverged at this point, but it is probably hardly noticeable in their life. Our brain tries to take our circumstances, and make them feel normal. However strange our circumstances are (and everyone's are to some extent), then providing they're ok, they can feel normal to us.

Next they join a second social group. The behaviours they use in the first social group were copied from those around them, because their natural behaviours are more associated with their inherited level. When they apply these new, copied behaviours to the second social group, they find they aren't quite as accepted. The second group is quite different to the first, despite being at the same level in society, and it is different enough that the person struggles to be treated as if they were of the same level. This feels bad, not being treated according to their identity level, and the person retreats from this group, and is drawn back to the first social group more strongly.

They then find a third social group, at a similar level, with people that they feel more comfortable with. That group is similar to the first, so their behaviours integrate, and they are able to be treated according to their identity, and being diverged isn't a problem.

The person may find it harder to interact with their old school friends, because their identity level has increased since then, and they now judge others from a "higher level". Whilst they may try to interact with old friends at a "lower level" how they once did, it becomes a little harder, and they'll perhaps come across as a little patronising. Also it's also unlikely those old friends will fully recognise that the person they once knew, and felt similar to, now feels at a higher level.

There are many ways a life can turn, but in each case it follows similar rules or patterns. We adopt the identity from the highest group that we've found acceptance in, and our identity can only go up. If we find it hard to maintain that identity, we feel frustrated and it can be hurtful, and we still try to hold onto it.

Our identity level can jump up quite quickly. If we find acceptance, then it doesn't take long for our brain to latch onto that, and absorb it as our new self-definition.

However, even if we don't move up or down in society, or groups, then because each person is diverged in modern societies, due to the difficult social environment we find ourselves in (the "social delta"), the question is not if someone is diverged, but how much they are.

Levels scenario

In order to understand our inherited level, we can consider a family tree. Our inherited level comes from our family, and therefore to understand it better we have to look at what can be going on in a family over time.

Our inherited level comes from our parents, because we subconsciously copy their interactions and emotions, and at least a part of our parents wants us to be a reflection of themselves. Therefore how our levels compare to our parents' levels can affect the parent-child dynamic, which can be important, and can sometimes affect how a person behaves in the social groups and hierarchies they are a part of.

We all find ourselves in slightly different places in society, and more so the more multi-layered and unequal our societies are. We then have a contrast between the family dynamic, where the parent is the parent, and the societal dynamic, where the parent and child have (often different) identity levels within society. The parent and child can have very different identity levels, i.e. different status groups they feel accepted in. Each will be drawing definition, and sense of belonging, from those different groups (potentially at different levels), and the parent-child relationship has to fit against this somehow.

How our identity level compares to our parents' identity level(s), and how the inherited levels rumble on beneath, can play a big part in the parent-child relationship, as well as to reinforce the characteristics of levels themselves.

To explore this, below is a diagram showing a fictional example of 5 generations of the same family. Each person is shown with their inherited level, which they've absorbed from their parents (and which is fairly constant throughout their own life), and their identity level, which is the maximum level they achieved in their life.

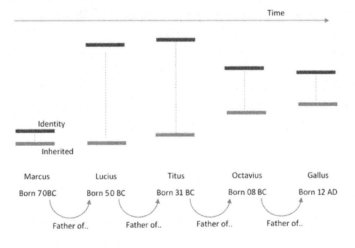

This is just one example of what could happen over five generations. This example, and ones like it, are one of many possible patterns that have played out down generations, for 12,000 years, ever since we gave up our hunter-gatherer lifestyles. It is an example of how our large societies can cause our three main drivers: family; group; and our desire to maximise our value; to head in different directions, whilst our self and emotions are still being dictated by each of them.

This example could therefore be from a family in ancient Maya, the early Shang dynasty in China, Renaissance Italy, Romanov Russia, or, the modern day. In this example, I have chosen this brief story of 5 generations to be set in the Roman empire.

However, before delving into this scenario, to look at how the levels affected their lives, we need to understand a few basic principles of how levels affect the interactions between parent and child, as well as how levels affect each person's experiences of the world.

And, as a side note, whilst interactions caused by levels play out across any age, but tend to have most impact once the child has reached adulthood and our personalities become more solidified. In the English language, we don't have a variety of different words that distinguish between adolescent children, adult children, and children of any age. "Offspring" is a little impersonal, so I use the word "child" simply to mean a person of any age, when discussing them in relation to their parent. Therefore where I use the word "child", it can mean a young person or adult person.

The effects of levels on our life

Parents

How our levels compare to our parents can have a big impact on the dynamic.

In our huge societies, people move around a lot, and it tests the simple parent-child mechanisms. Often a certain amount of restraint is applied from the parent because of this. Parenthood can become a balancing act between encouraging children, and limiting them, so that they are someone we can (theoretically) pass on love and affection to.

We all want to have supportive parents, and to be good parents ourselves. Yet in the modern world this relationship is a difficult one at the best of times. Difficulty gets complicated, and manifests itself down generations, but conflict, between parent and child, is often related (somewhere or another) to levels, and how diverged we all are.

It's difficult as a child to understand that our parents are acting according to levels. Instead we are generally blindsided by quite core emotional needs. Levels are perhaps more apparent to parents, whilst they become irrelevant, or secondary, from the child's perspective.

It is often better not to get too deep into the ins and outs of our parents, it is not necessary for feeling good about the world, nor managing difficulty. Often it is easier and better to focus on a purpose or something that represents our individuality, to find our way in life. However, the parental relationship does tend to underly our world, and occasionally rear its head. And sometimes we have to face it, perhaps when things go awry. Even if we don't, if we can find some better understanding of what's going on there, we can take one step closer to them, and perhaps give us a better understanding of ourselves, and who we are.

Both the relative identity levels, and relative inherited levels, can affect the parent-child dynamic.

The identity and inherited levels are passed to the child through everything the parent does, good and bad. These two levels are deeply ingrained in the parent, as they are in any human being, and so they are passed on to the child in all of their interactions. This is why a relationship between a parent and child is so personal, because how the child feels about the parent comes down to a multitude of tiny interactions across our life, that in some ways represent the inherited level and the identity level.

We feel a need to replicate out parent's identity level.

Even when our parents don't directly put pressure on us, there can be some pressure to attain an identity level that isn't below our parents. Conversely, if we exceed the parent's identity level, then they will reduce us a little in order that we don't judge ourselves as above them. These forces, on both sides, are quite strong, as they come from our core drivers, each of which has a powerful influence on us.

We are also passed our parent's inherited level.

This occurs by subconsciously picking up on how our parents respond to the world around us. We see how our parents react to people and places, and something deep in our brains replicates that in ourselves. This is the part of us that is learning socialisation from the parent, and how the parent is playing the role of the social anchor. It can be frustrating at times. For example, sometimes we find our parent's responses to others annoying, for example when they appear nervous around people we want to associate with. If they were confident with those people, perhaps we'd find it easier to be.

Our inherited level can often also be transferred through more direct action from the parents, which the parent does in order to ensure that their child doesn't have greater social freedom in the world than them. If the child had more freedom, the child would be a much greater threat to the parent in any conflict between them, which would cause the parent to be less kind, open and loving, as they acted to maintain some authority.

In the modern world, the levels we receive can often be a little mismatched. It's not our parents' fault, their levels came from their parents, and theirs from our great grandparents, and so on, but it can mean we are sometimes trying to achieve an identity level against a inherited level that doesn't quite fit.

If our parents are diverged themselves, as most modern humans are, to some extent, it will look something like this:

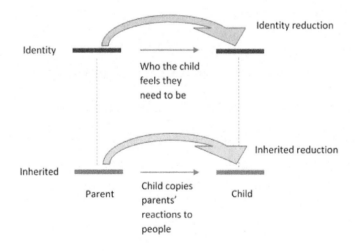

The large arrows in the diagram imply some sort of downward, limiting force. In some respects this is true. Some limitation will come from society, from what we can achieve against our inherited position, but a fair amount comes from the parent, inevitably. This is because the parent, instinctively, has to maintain some authority, against a world where the child could "out-value" them. The more unequal society is, the greater chance there is for a child to "out-value" the parent, so the more restrictive the parent has to be. It is frustrating for the child to be limited. In the modern world, these forces, to pass down positions and behaviours from parent to child, are playing out in an unnatural environment.

These downward arrows act on both the inherited level, and the identity level. Some of this will be subconscious, for example the child picking up on the parents' reactions and projections of themselves, and mirroring them somewhat, and others will be more through actions, and the parent-child dynamic, for example the parent verbalising how the child might react, or influencing who the child feels they are.

You can see in the above diagram the parent is diverged, and so the child will be diverged too. The child's levels tend to mirror (or at least be guided by) the parent's.

From this, we can start to see how levels play a part in the dynamic. In reality, in other examples, there can be much greater differences between child and parent, which can cause peculiar and difficult conflicts, as we shall explore in the Roman scenario.

Before looking at how our levels affect our personal life experiences, it's worth noting a point about adulthood.

We have lifelong bonds with our parents. We often, given the nature of difficult parent-child relationships, like to think we are independent, free and distant from our parent's influence as an adult. We can be, and we are to some extent. But our emotions retain some tie to them. Our programming treats them as the anchor for learning during adolescence, and they remain so in adulthood.

When we reach adulthood, and our own personality and identity firms up, the parent-child relationship can be harder. We both have our fixed points, which are often in different places, and defined in different circumstances and sub-cultures. Deviating from our identities (the place our personality has settled in) can be hard. This leads to some distance and conflict, which means that when we want support from our parents, which we all do from time to time, as we find our way as an adult (or when we have children ourselves), we can't access it. We can find that that desire for support conflicts with a need to be independent.

This is representative of the difficulty in living in large civilisations, compared to the hunter-gatherer tribe. There, we'd grow into our parents' position in the tribe, passing rites of passage, and gaining their approval as a fully-fledged adult, alongside our parents. We'd have support when we needed it, without feeling less for asking. It is easy to help someone walk a path that we have walked ourself.

Ourself

We've absorbed some levels from our parent, and then we have to face the world by ourselves.

In doing so, in socialising, competing, and finding our way, we have our own two levels: our inherited level and our identity level. Depending on where we find ourself in the world, they can differ greatly from person to person, but one common thing we can look at, which defines a lot about that person's personal experiences, is how far apart those two levels are, i.e. how diverged a person is.

Being more diverged as a human can (not always, but can) make our lives a little more difficult.

This is because how we emotionally respond to people and environments, and how we feel we should be responding, are different. We have to work harder on our self-beliefs, change behaviours to compensate, and perhaps find a deeper sense of support in society, in order to maintain our identity level.

Part of the reason for this is that like it or not, we are tied to our inherited level. We may not always feel it, we may develop behaviours that circumvent it, or find situations where we can avoid feeling it, but our evolutionary programming means it can't really change.

It's like we're all on a mountainside. We have a rope tied to us, that is linked to an anchor point (our inherited level). The rope is stretchy and elastic, so we can move up and down the mountain, in between and around other people. At times the rope is slack and we don't notice it. Occasionally however the rope tightens a bit and pulls us towards the anchor. The further we've climbed, the more it might pull. We can resist it, but it takes energy to do so.

It means that when someone challenges us, and adds a little extra weight for us to carry, because we are already fighting a pull from our rope to our anchor, then resisting or responding to that challenge is a little harder.

Below is a less diverged person facing four challenges over a period of time, with time flowing from left to right:

The challenges are when someone has said or taken action against us, as part of the difficult social environment we face, perhaps at work, in our families, or amongst our friends.

When our thoughts and feelings are below our identity level, we don't feel ourselves. We feel demeaned, denied a feeling of fulfilment, and feel angry or frustrated.

In the above example, the inherited level is actually helping us recover from the challenge. It isn't too far away from the identity level, so when people knock us down the mountainside, our elastic rope actually pulls us back upwards, and we get on with our lives.

The person will be annoyed, upset or frustrated by the challenge, but they will soon forget about it.

In contrast, here is how a more diverged person responds to the same set of challenges:

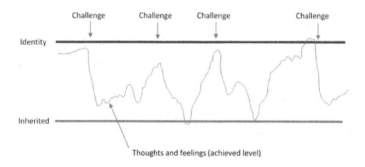

You can see how the challenges have a much greater impact, because of the difference between the inherited and identity levels. That rope, tied below us on the mountainside, makes it much harder to maintain our footing in the jostling world of the level we find ourselves at. We have to expend more energy recovering from the challenge, and maintaining our identity.

As the diverged person is more affected by the same challenges, they need more people to draw on as a source of positive definition, for getting themselves back to their identity, and perhaps greater influence over these people.

There is huge variation in how this plays out from person to person. Some people are largely diverged, but find good environments, where they aren't challenged very often. Others face more competitive environments, where they have more of a daily battle. In both cases the situation is the same though, and when the challenge does come in, the more diverged person will have a harder time recovering from it, in order to be their identity level.

People being diverged is an inevitable side-effect of unequal societies. As people deal with being diverged, they level the playing field. Greater divergence is associated with greater social mobility, which helps bring society towards a common point.

However, what is good for society isn't always good for an individual. In our own lives, being diverged can mean fighting battles on an unequal playing field. Say the two people in the examples above are trying to achieve the same identity level, for example they are colleagues who are working together. For the more diverged person, it is harder. They are facing the same things, but are feeling more of a reaction to it, and a greater headwind. They see themselves as the same identity level, and don't want extra help or sympathy. Nevertheless, the playing field they are both interacting on isn't actually level, and it's bumpy and has ridges and divots. And often those ridges and divots are hidden, invisible, or well-disguised.

Therefore, to be diverged can make our lives more difficult. We can face a greater headwind in achieving similar results to the people around us. In overcoming this, we level the playing field, and the people that follow have an easier time being a human being.

With an idea of how levels affect the parent-child relationship, and how they affect an individual's life experiences, we can then look at how the scenario of five Roman generations plays out.

Levels scenario

Heading back to Rome.

It's 55 BC and Julius Caesar landed on the shores of Britain for the first time. Before then, Britain was a myth, a faraway land. Nobody from Rome had ever been there, and the second-hand stories the Romans heard, about the indigenous people, were exaggerated myths of druids and savage warriors covered in blue warpaint. For Julius to land on the shores of Britain was like landing on the moon at the time, and so it was an impressive feat, that elevated his cult following[21].

Julius was a smart self-promotor, and was ambitious. He sent home stories of his exploits that were told by orators on the streets of Rome, often with a few embellishments in order to further his celebrity. At this time, he was head of the army, and yet to become dictator of Rome, but was amassing popularity and support with every military victory he had across the landscape of Europe.

Marcus, who lived in a small town outside of Rome, was 15 years old when this happened, and Julius was instantly his hero. He played around the local cobbled streets outside his parent's modest home, brandishing a wooden sword and shield. As his father was a blacksmith, he was the envy of his friends with a replica legionnaires belt.

Marcus grew up to be a blacksmith himself, following in his father's footsteps. His life, and the lives of four generations that came after him, can serve as an example of how inherited position and identity can change from one generation to the next.

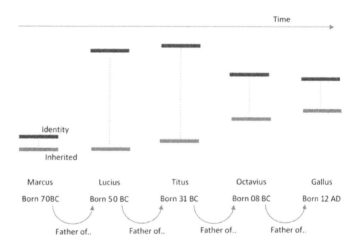

This example follows the male half of the family, but it could equally be applied to the female half of the family too, or with some intermixing. We tend to be more influenced by family members of the same sex, since on average there are more similarities, but every situation is different.

Applying the theory from the previous section, we can now assess how the changing levels, of the five generations of his fictional family, played out in the relationships, and to the people themselves.

Marcus learnt his trade from his father, in the family business. Life is fairly straightforward for Marcus, he is popular among the townsfolk, and after work he often went to the town forum to have a few drinks with his friends, who he'd grown up with. He felt content, and himself.

His inherited level was similar to his identity level. He was playing a part similar to his father, as well as a few generations before that. How he reacted to people was similar to who he felt he was. He was happy in his life, but gave little thought to the world around him, they didn't bother him and he didn't bother them. Despite the changing world (Julius Caesar had become dictator in 45BC, and was assassinated in 44BC), Marcus was relatively unaffected. Blacksmithing was a trade in demand, and his life wasn't strongly impacted by the social and political landscape.

Marcus fell in love with a local girl who he'd always had a crush on, and they had two surviving children, a boy Lucius and a girl Aurelia. At the time infant mortality was high, and Marcus had lost three children. He often thought about them, and wondered what type of people they'd grow up to be.

His children Lucius and Aurelia were quite different. Lucius was academic whilst his sister was artistic. Marcus wanted Lucius to follow him into the family business of blacksmithing, but whilst Lucius showed an interest, he was also finding success in school. He was good with numbers, and enjoyed maths.

Marcus tried to praise Lucius for his maths work, but it didn't seem to work. He didn't feel his praise for maths really felt genuine, and this seemed to push Lucius away more. One day a recruiter from the Roman Imperial treasury came to the school, to give a talk on accounts, and explained how a *rationarium* was being prepared, listing all of Rome's finances for the first time. In it would be public revenues, cash in the treasury, cash with tax officials and cash in public contractors[22]. The recruiter explained how this was revolutionary, and the next step in the development of their great civilisation. He wore fine clothes and jewellery, and carried an authority that made an impression on Lucius. Being good at maths, the recruiter talked to Lucius personally, and encouraged him to put in an application when he finished school at the end of the year. Lucius excitedly told his parents that evening. They tried to be supportive, but didn't seem to completely share his optimism, which annoyed Lucius.

Lucius did put in that application, and was successful. He moved to the city of Rome, and became an accountant. When he was leaving, his father was distant and didn't seem supportive, and Lucius got annoyed and they didn't part on the best terms. Marcus was pleased for his son's achievements, he wanted Lucius to follow his dreams, after all he remembered having dreams of his own, but it was going against his programming. It felt like Lucius thought blacksmithing wasn't good enough for him, or that he didn't look up to Marcus enough to follow in his footsteps. The path Lucius was following slightly intimidated Marcus. He wanted Lucius to find his own individuality, but that individuality was having ramifications.

After a while, Lucius was starting to challenge him in ways he wasn't used to, and he found himself more opposed. It wasn't that Marcus was easily intimidated, but Rome had always been a distant thought. He'd been there a few times, and didn't like the noise and bustle. He found Romans superior, and they had odd and different behaviours, and he always longed to go back to his home town.

But Lucius fitted in there. Accountants had good social standing in Rome. He was good at his job, and it felt rewarding, it felt as if he was making a difference to the world.

In 27 BC Augustus became the first Emperor, and the Roman Empire began in full force. It was an exciting and optimistic time to be a 23-year-old in the capital city. Lucius earned a good salary, more money than he'd ever seen, and bought nice clothes, pottery, and eventually a house in one of Rome's suburbs. Because of this, Lucius's identity level was that of a wealthy Roman accountant, who he felt was changing the world. He couldn't help but feel far above the small town he came from.

However, Lucius's inherited level was still similar to, and linked to, his fathers. Throughout his life, his brain had followed cues from how his parents reacted to other people, including those from the city of Rome. When his parents came to visit, they seemed nervous and out of place, and often made derogatory comments about the locals, and this frustrated Lucius. Lucius needed to associate with those around him as an equal, since that is his identity, and found it uncomfortable seeing his parents feel uncomfortable there.

Through this process the inherited level is transferred from parent to child, even in adulthood. Lucius' mind is picking up on, and replicating, his parent's reactions.

Lucius started to reject that he was similar to Marcus, and instead felt similar to the role models around him. Nevertheless, he found working with wealthy Romans, who'd grown up in the city, with their private tutors and large houses, a little intimidating. He was just as good at the job than them, but his inherited position was responding to them as if they were above him, whilst his identity was that they were equal. He found himself competing with them as if he was an equal, but found it was as if he was facing a greater headwind.

He made friends with someone similar to him at the business, who also came from a small town. He focussed deeply on his work, aiming for targets, and trying to get good appraisals. He became a team leader, not least due to his focus and attention to detail, and adopted the new position, and the behaviours that went with it, with some gusto. He enjoyed this, and those behaviours that he used at work, as a team leader, filtered into his personality. He met a wife at a chariot race he attended, with his friends, and they fell in love.

He fell out with his father Marcus. When Lucius walked into his old town wearing fine clothes, and acting like a manager, Marcus felt compelled to disapprove and reduce Lucius. He was still the father, and wanted the respect from that, and some authority, but instead found Lucius judging him from a superior position. Marcus wanted respect as a father and a blacksmith, whilst Lucius wanted support from Marcus, as well as to be treated as an elevated Roman accountant. Neither got what they wanted.

It might seem like this dynamic, and these reactions, are arbitrary, and perhaps that they could be overcome with a strong will, or a different approach. However, it goes deeper than that. If society is seated around a stadium, in some sort of social pecking order, then the different places in society, that Marcus and Lucius find themselves in, are like Lucius going and sitting in a different section of the stadium to his father. The dynamic, and social forces they experience, are representative of the thousands of people now seated between them. They are trying to have a parent-child relationship, whilst at different places in a society of millions.

Both were bitter and sad at this. Marcus felt that his son wasn't respecting him, and was frustrated that he couldn't show love and affection. It was also frustrating for Marcus because he couldn't fathom Lucius' point of view. After all, Marcus was an upstanding member of his town, and had many friends, but that wasn't enough for Lucius. Every now and again he would try to praise Lucius for being an accountant, but it just didn't come off right, and seemed to annoy Lucius more.

Lucius felt frustrated because his father wasn't approving of him, nothing he did was good enough for Marcus. Lucius couldn't understand Marcus' behaviour, he felt Marcus should be pleased and proud of him for his achievements, but it wasn't felt.

This is what levels can do, and what happens when the parental driver, the group driver, and the drive to maximise our value, become out of balance. Both want what they feel they should get from a father or son, but that now conflicts with the situation in front of them.

In relation to modern hierarchies, the point is that the hierarchies are full of people all having these complex personal lives, often with a split between who they feel they are, how they come across, and what they want. People all around us can be diverged through unusual circumstances, whilst experiencing the consequences and trying to fit loose-ends together.

With our spread-out social lives, and the possibility of divergence, then in order to really understand groups, you have to consider more than what is going on on the surface. Individuals in a group have complex situations and needs, often driven by levels and divergence.

For example, because of Lucius' circumstances, he found work occasionally stressful, and often conflicts at work caused him to spend a whole evening frustrated. He sought dependence more deeply in his wife, who helped him reaffirm that he deserved to be there, which he did, his work was very good. Occasionally he showed his frustration at work, and found himself blaming others in his business for sometimes minor mistakes, and sometimes, in private, blaming his father for making his life difficult.

The parent-child dynamic between Lucius and Marcus is very difficult to resolve. It is down to levels, which always complicate situations. The social dynamic, driven by groups, and the desire to maximise our value, are in direct conflict with the parental driver.

Marcus can't admit to Lucius that he is at a higher level. Lucius can't let Marcus treat him as below him, with authority, as a son.

Even if Marcus could somehow be entirely supportive, Lucius is actually battling his own inherited level, which neither Marcus nor Lucius can have a say over. Lucius' levels, including his inherited level, (which is derived from Marcus, whether either of them likes it or not), are what Lucius has to face the world against. Lucius finds increased frustration at having to maintain an identity level distant from his inherited level, and because the inherited level is drawn from the parent, the frustration often manifests itself in that direction.

There are many ways this can resolve, and many compromises that can be reached. Occasionally, when things are going well, he and Marcus get along. Lucius feels he has a good life, and feels fortunate. He has broken the mould, and played a part in the intermixing of Roman society, but neither of those are easy, and the reason for that comes down to levels.

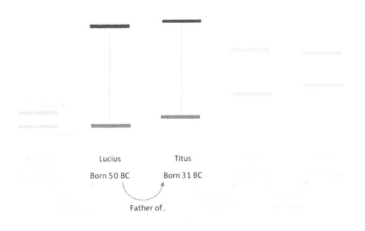

Lucius   Titus

Born 50 BC   Born 31 BC

Father of..

Lucius had three surviving children, a boy, Titus, and two girls, Cecilia and Livia. His children grew up in the suburb of Rome, very different to Lucius' upbringing as a small-town blacksmith's son. Titus grew up with all the privilege and wealth of the son of a Roman accountant. His father Lucius had grown up as the son of a blacksmith.

As such, Titus' inherited level was higher than Lucius'. But it was only a little above Lucius'. Even though Lucius' identity was as a fully-fledged, moderately wealthy citizen of Rome, having spent his adult life there as an accountant, his son Titus' human brain picked up on the fact that Lucius was reacting to people as if they were above him. This would happen both consciously and subconsciously, for example by watching the difficulty that Lucius experience in his life and work.

Not only this, but Lucius didn't want Titus to feel completely at ease in the environment, because he didn't. If Titus was at ease, he would have a distinct advantage in any conflict between them. This conflict can come from, for example, when Titus was a teenager. As teenagers we try out new behaviours, and test our parents a little, which is part of our mechanism for ensuring interaction, and forcing levels to be passed down. In modern societies, where we have to reduce our children a little more than we needed to as hunter-gatherers, this can lead to more conflict. So Lucius, even though he didn't want to, felt compelled to make his son Titus a little less secure. This is how the inherited level is passed from Lucius to Titus.

This was confusing for Titus. His father Lucius projected himself at one level, but didn't quite give Titus the support to achieve it himself. As a result they were not emotionally close. When Titus faced difficulty, his father didn't seem to really understand, and instead encouraged him to focus on achieving success in his career in order to solve his problems. Titus found that he saw his father one way, but his father spoke as if he was something else. When, occasionally, Titus opened up to Lucius, he found Lucius talk to him from a level that he didn't feel he justified, which felt uncomfortable. As a father, Lucius often was distant with Titus, as if he was protecting something.

They were amicable, but Titus moved to the other side of Rome, blocked out some of Lucius' behaviour in his mind, and instead had a very close-knit group of friends, who enjoyed Roman theatre and comedy.

Lucius was even a little derogatory towards his son's friendship group. Lucius wasn't a part of such a group himself, as he had always felt a little of an outsider, and felt a little threatened by Titus' acceptance there.

It was tolerable. Titus was finding success, as an architect specialising in aqueduct building. The Roman Empire was entering the Pax Romana, a period of 200 years of relative peace and stability, and there were plenty of aqueducts to be built. Titus travelled across Italy and even into Europe with his job, and thus obtained a similar identity level to his father Lucius. Lucius was proud of Titus. He told his accountant friends of children's successes, and they became competitive over them. But he found it very difficult to praise or show this to Titus, and instead kept him at arm's length.

When we're diverged, it can be difficult being emotionally close to people. This is because we want two things: we want them to see us at our *identity level*, which is who we feel we are; but we also want them to support us and understand our *inherited level*, which is how we're responding to the world (and often the cause of our difficulty). These two things are often incompatible. The closer people are to us, the more they see and experience our emotional reactions, and how we see the world, which is our inherited level. If our inherited level is a long way from our identity level, we often are quite guarded of it, since if it is exposed, it can be harder to maintain our identity level.

Children, who want to be emotionally close to their parents, and who are noticing and copying their parent's emotional responses, are exposed to their parent's inherited positions much more than the average person on the street. As a parent we sense this, and can sometimes keep our children at arm's-length, to keep our inherited level defended, and our identity level maintained.

All these mechanisms are part of a cascade, that, one way or another, causes traits and behaviours to be passed from parent to child. Titus felt that he was quite different to his father, yet because Lucius was diverged, Titus was also diverged. Due to levels, Lucius had never received comfortable praise from his father Marcus, and so he found it hard to give to Titus. Because Lucius focussed on his job and career, Titus also found himself focussed on his job and career.

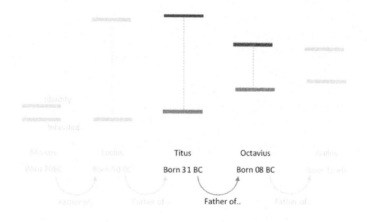

Titus married, and had a son Octavius. Titus wanted to be a better father to Octavius than Lucius had been to him, but as

Octavius grew up, he found himself doing some of the things Lucius had done.

Octavius' inherited level was a little higher than Titus', because they'd been living in the suburbs of Rome for two generations now, so it just seemed more comfortable to Octavius. Nevertheless, Titus still found that occasionally he had to make life a little more uncomfortable for Octavius, to match his own subconscious feelings.

Titus' primary focus in life was his close group of friends, who's main interest was the latest plays and comedies that travelling actors would perform. As a group they were a good collection of respectable individuals, and it formed quite a large part of how Titus felt about himself. He felt sure Octavius would look up to him when Octavius made his own friendship group. However, when it came to it, Octavius' became friends with a different kind of group. They were more outgoing, and enjoyed fighting like gladiators, and going to the local games. The Coliseum of Rome wasn't to be built for another 70 years, but still there were many games going on, and it was a part of Roman society. Octavius didn't look up to Titus how he thought he would, and they fell out as a result.

Octavius didn't have the aptitude for maths or design, that his father Titus did (or his grandfather accountant Lucius did), and so took a less well-paid job as a games designer. He enjoyed this greatly, as he got to work with designing sets and challenges for gladiators to face. But he just didn't feel Titus really appreciated him. Titus wanted to show it, but couldn't. When he tried to say how good he thought Octavius' games were, it just didn't sound right, and Octavius found it patronising. How Octavius' *identity level* compares to Titus' can have an influence on the dynamic, regardless of intent or goodwill (although efforts to show approval are always welcomed in the long run).

Octavius and Titus weren't emotionally close. Titus tried to project it, but it was clear his focus and behaviours were strongly tied to his friends. As his son, Octavius could sense that Titus was diverged, and that his reactions didn't quite match his identity. Whenever he was open with his father Titus, it always felt like Titus ignored those reactions and instead talked down to him, as if those insecurities didn't exist. If Octavius pointed this out, Titus became distant and defensive. To an individual, there is only one level: the identity level. To Titus, he was one and the same as his group of friends, and the idea that he felt unease at that level was inconceivable, at least to admit. Octavius felt he had to face a headwind in life (which he saw markedly in his dad Titus, due to the large divergence), whilst pretending those headwinds didn't exist (like his dad Titus).

Octavius enjoyed his work, and despite the conflict with Titus, had a good life. He lived to a relatively old age for the time, just long enough to see the building of the great Coliseum, which filled Octavius with excitement and marvel.

Octavius had married, and had a son Gallus. Octavius and Gallus were closer than any of the previous generations. Gallus' inherited level was consistent with a citizen of Rome living in the suburbs, as his family had been living there for four generations. He had friends and a job similar to his father Octavius, and so was more comfortable in life. He found his father Octavius difficult at times: Octavius never quite felt good enough, and so treated Gallus in a similar way. However, Octavius was more open with Gallus, and able to explain his situation, and so Gallus was able to live with the relationship more easily than some of the generations before.

Octavius   Gallus

Born 08 BC   Born 12 AD

Father of..

Of all the generations, Octavius and Gallus had the most similar levels. It meant that Gallus, like his great, great, grandfather Marcus, had a place in life that matched his father, and likely behaviours and traits to go along with it. Perhaps Gallus had the most comfortable life. Perhaps Gallus was the "best" son, and perhaps Octavius is the "best" father, but neither are fair statements. There is so much out of our control when levels become involved, and much of it comes down to chance and circumstance.

It took four generations for the strong divergence, that Lucius experienced, to be lessened, and for the inherited level to slowly rise, one generation to the next, so that Gallus actually felt comfortable as a citizen of Rome's suburbs. This was just a small jump too, there are much bigger jumps out there.

It is easy to describe a fictional example of five generations in a short passage, and see the contrast and developments, but, if it reflects reality, then for each of those generations, one of those unique circumstances was their whole life. We may be one of those generations, unaware that our circumstances may have been dictated by events several generations ago, and that our relationship with our parents perhaps bears the hallmarks of the relationship between our great grandparent and their parents.

Each of the people within that story will have been part of many hierarchies. How they fitted into, and interacted within those hierarchies will have been affected by their identity and inherited levels, which are quite complex factors. For example they can include any or all of the difficulties discussed in this chapter, and that then feeds into the unusual interactions between people in groups, as discussed in Chapter 4. This will be going on all around society, and it means modern hierarchies are full of interacting people that may be facing internal quandaries, or difficulties, that affect how they feel about the world and the groups that they are a part of.

This story of five generations is just one example of what *can* happen and why. It is representative of the forces felt by modern humans, and how they play out on our lives. Any difficulty felt can be greater or less from person to person due to a large range of factors. Sometimes issues arise that are a cause of great difficulty, and sometimes there is some fortune involved and the difficulty is never exposed. Even with difficulty, which everyone feels to some extent, we can find happiness in our lives, levels are certainly not a barrier to that.

Should Marcus have prevented Lucius from taking that job, and following his dreams?

Would Lucius have thanked Marcus for preventing him becoming an accountant, even if Lucius could have had a comfortable life as a blacksmith?

Even if he knew how it eventually panned out, would Lucius have chosen to be a blacksmith, and missed out on the chance to know what it's like to live as a citizen of Rome, own expensive clothes, and know what it feels like to be at the forefront of the developing world?

In each case, probably not. There's perhaps little that could have stopped Lucius resisting the draw to maximise his value. It would be quite hard for a person to deny themselves the opportunity to feel success and elevation, even if they knew it would come with difficulty.

The impact on the lives of these five generations are a result of each generation's inherited level and identity level, and how those levels compare to their parents. The circumstances of Lucius' divergence caused impacts down the generations. We see this all around society. We can't help being diverged as modern humans, and it is more a case of *how* diverged we are. And, as we have seen, and perhaps you believe (or not), it can have a big influence on our relationship with our parents, and our experiences of the world.

The social delta

The final topic to look at is why *everyone* is diverged. As we have seen throughout this book, modern hierarchies are defined by the fact that people can have identities that are perhaps inconsistent with their inherited levels.

We have seen how people can diverge in their lifetimes to increase their identity level, but this doesn't explain why everyone is diverged. In order to understand that, we have to consider the "social delta".

The social delta is the reason why the vast majority of human beings, who live in large societies, are diverged.

The social delta lowers the inherited level of each person, so that they face an additional headwind in maintaining their identity. Every person's inherited position then becomes more of an unwelcome inconvenience.

The larger the society, and the greater the inequality in it, the larger the social delta.

In a tribe, levels are merely about position. If we adopt the same position in the tribe as a few generations of our family beforehand, we will not be diverged at all. We will feel entirely comfortable in that position, and have a set of natural behaviours that fit it. Our identity level, who we feel we are, and our inherited level, how we emotionally react to those around us, are the same.

In large societies, our levels are about positions **plus** the social delta. Even if we adopt exactly the same status in society, and the same social position in our friendship groups, compared to several generations of our family before us, we will still be diverged a little. Each person faces additional headwinds to simply feeling fulfilled in a comfortable social position (assuming we even have a comfortable position).

Large societies cause a social delta for two main reasons. One is the spread of our social lives across several groups, and the other is inequality, which gives rise to the possibility that the child can "out-value" the parent.

In terms of having social lives spread over several groups, this causes additional headwind because each group has a slightly different sub-culture. They may have their own cliquey language, their own jokes, things they value, enjoy doing, and things they don't, and disapprove of. There will be groups we feel better represent us, but it's unlikely we'll have a group that completely matches our values and interests. Given our social lives are spread over several groups, we will often come across groups that have different sub-cultures to the ones we are most comfortable in. Therefore, at least parts of our social lives will contain greater hesitancy and reservations about truly expressing ourselves. Or, if we express ourselves without reservations, then we may face resistance and conflict from time to time.

Even in the groups that best represent us, with our closest friends, we may have to bend and adapt our views, values and interests to fit in. Perhaps some of ourselves fits better in one group, and a different part of our individuality fits in another, but it's rare for all of ourself to be truly represented in one group.

Compare this to a tribe, it is more likely that our views, values and interests grow in unison with all the people that we integrate with, since we stay with that one group our whole lives. Who we grow into, fits what we grow into.

However, perhaps more importantly, our spread-out social lives (and the difference in sub-culture from one group to the next) affect the parent-child relationship.

In large societies, when children grow, and find groups that represent them, it is likely that these groups don't include their parents. The child absorbs the sub-culture and behaviours of those groups, and, it's likely that those sub-cultures and behaviours differ from the ones their parents feel most comfortable in. In any parent-child relationship, there will be some conflict, and the child will challenge the parent, whether in finding boundaries, finding individuality as a teenager, or establishing themselves as an adult. If they challenge the parent from the viewpoint of a sub-culture the parent doesn't recognise, or behaviours the parent isn't comfortable with, then the parent will reduce the child more than they would otherwise.

The parent has to reduce the child in this way, in order to maintain authority, despite the differing sub-cultures and behaviours of their respective identities. The parent reduces the child to ensure the child isn't too comfortable in sub-cultures very different from the parent's. If the child was, then the parent would have a harder time maintaining their position of authority, which their core drivers, and deep instincts, encourage them not to yield.

On the second reason for the social delta: inequality, this also affects the parent-child relationship, because there now exists the possibility that our children can "out-value" us.

If they attain acceptance in a higher group, then their group driver causes them to feel a part of that group, and feel similar to, and a reflection of, the people in it. They judge others from the viewpoint of that group. They expect to be treated consistent with how someone else of that group is treated. When they apply these to the parent-child relationship, they can then look down on the parent. They are being pulled towards a position higher than the parent, whilst the parent is trying to maintain the upper hand themselves.

The parent naturally tries to maintain authority. This results in a situation where, against the mere possibility that the child can "out-value" the parent, the parent has to apply extra restraint, in order to balance their authority as a parent, with the social position that their child may attain.

The greater the inequality in society, the more restraint the parent may have to apply.

They have to apply greater constraint and caution (alongside encouragement), in order to prevent their children being drawn towards the top, and becoming someone that they can't interact with: someone that looks down on them.

Greater inequality also affects the first reason for the social delta (our spread-out social lives).

The more unequal a society is, the more people have to gain and lose. This causes people to seek greater security in groups. Groups become more cliquey and insular. If the mountainside is steeper, and those below (or above) us are driven by a greater desire to usurp us (or resist us), then we seek greater security in closer friendships. The sub-cultures of individual groups become more different and distinct, in order to provide that security.

The result of each group being more distinct is that it is less likely that they fully represent us, and we have to bend further to fit into a narrower set of views. Also, it raises the chances that a child's sub-culture, that they feel most comfortable in, and that represents them, is different from their parent's. This increases the constraint and reduction that the parent has to apply in order to maintain authority. This in turn leads to a lower inherited level, and therefore a greater headwind to achieving an identity level.

Therefore the greater inequality in society, the greater the social delta.

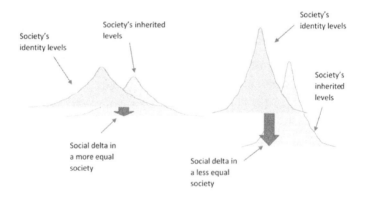

The cause of the social delta (that is causing everyone to be diverged), is our spread-out social lives, and the possibility of a child "out-valuing" the parent. Both reasons are exacerbated by greater inequality in society.

The social delta has its source in the parent-child relationship. As parents try to be parents, against an unequal society of spread-out groups, they apply additional constraint, which causes additional divergence. Humans then find they are trying to be "complete", and feel fulfilled, against a difficult social backdrop, and without the full support of the parent.

To each individual, we then find an additional headwind in being our identity. For example, we may only feel ourselves, and be treated according to our identity level, in pockets. In certain groups, we do, in others, it can be a fight to be treated how we want. Often, even in our closest groups, it can be a fight to be treated according to what we feel is our identity.

This is the "social delta". Positions aside, each person will feel an additional headwind to being their identity level. On average, the social delta is lowering the inherited levels of each person. The larger and more unequal a society is, the more this is the case.

This is why, as modern humans living in large societies, the question is not whether someone is diverged, but how much.

6

Summary

Modern hierarchies are much more complicated than they should be. As discussed in this book, this comes down to two main factors. One is that the variety of competition has increased, and the other is that people can face a split between who they feel they are (their identity level) and how they respond to the world around them (their inherited level): they can be diverged.

When people are diverged, it can create unusual conflicts and group structures, as observed in Chapter 4. It can also create internal conflicts for the individual, as discussed in Chapter 5, which in turn affect the group further. A large part of the unusual nature of modern hierarchies comes down to this idea of divergence, proposed in this book. A person can have a difference between their identity level and their inherited level, and this is one of the defining aspects of modern groups.

Therefore "levels" (identity and inherited) are one of the key takeaways of the topics discussed.

The levels that we have, in the various hierarchies that we

are a part of, are very important to us, whether considered against an individual, a group, a parent-child relationship, or across society. They represent something tangible, a pecking order, that is something that is key throughout nature. As these pecking orders exist, so they must have an effect on us, and drive our behaviours and emotions.

Levels represent our desire to maximise our value, and survival of the fittest. They represent our driver to draw definition and identity from a group, to become part of it, and act in unison with it. They represent our driver to draw learning from, and follow, the generations before us. They represent our need to be anchored. They represent the part of us is fixed, and part of us is flexible. They represent the fact that we can adapt to the world around us, but fundamentally remain human, and display the same characteristics that caused our species to become so widespread, and arguably successful, in the past.

However, whilst levels are tangible, the way we experience them isn't. Whilst they drive much of the behaviour around us, we generally don't see it that way. We experience levels in an obscure, indirect way, and often our focus, attention, and understanding are diverted onto conflicts in front of us, that appear unique and unrelated. Our brains are very good at assessing and acting according to levels, but our conscious thought tends to be diverted and caught up on conflicts and experiences in the foreground instead (this is explored more in the larger companion book "A Theory of Everyone", also by John Almeryn).

Finally, we have our own levels.

We have our inherited level, that defines how we react to the world around us. We generally ignore this in ourselves, and believe we only have our identity level. Nevertheless, we draw this inherited level mainly from our parents, by copying their reactions to people around us, but it also in a small part tempered by the world we grow into.

Then we have our identity level, that generally revolves around the maximum status group we are a part of. It is normally found in a pocket of our life, and we generally try to bend our social situations, that we have on a daily basis, to be more favourable to it.

In the modern world, our inherited level and identity level can be far apart, and we can be diverged. As we saw, most people are diverged, hence why we can only achieve our identity level in pockets. The more difficult the social environment, for example caused by greater inequality or complexity in society, the more diverged each person will be. The more difficult the social environment, the more each person (including our parents) faces a greater headwind between their inherited and identity level, and a has a harder time finding places where they truly feel themselves.

Modern hierarchies are often inconvenient and frustrating. They are full of people who may be diverged. They are full of people who may appear to think one thing, but present another, or come across one way, but find that hard to accept. Everyone has very complex circumstances, from competing forces (probably much more so than they realise), and this feeds into group dynamics. But this is the world around us, and this is the nature of modern hierarchies.

To understand ourselves, others, and what is going on in the world, we have to at least consider the topics discussed in this book, and how strong a driver they can be to human behaviour. They form a part of the modern human experience, often playing out in unusual and complex ways.

Notes

1 For the history of Charles Darwin, and *The Origin of Species*, see *Voyage of the Beagle*, first published in 1905, which details his journal during the voyage. Also see www.nhm.ac.uk/discover/charles-darwin-most-famous-biologist.html. For the history of London's air pollution, including during the industrial revolution, see https://ourworldindata.org/london-air-pollution and https://www.historic-uk.com/HistoryUK/HistoryofBritain/Timeline-Industrial-Revolution/.

2 In this book, discussion of early man (and historical dates in general), taken from Richard Overy *The Times Complete History of the World* (Times Books; Eighth edition, 2010), as well as Andrew Marr *A History of the World* (Pan Books, 2013) and Yuval Noah Harari *Sapiens: A Brief History of Humankind* (Vintage, 2015).

3 See Emily E. Groopman, Rachel N. Carmody and Richard W. Wrangham "Cooking increases net energy gain from a lipid-rich food" *Am J Phys Anthropol* (January 2015), 156(1): 11–18, which also discusses other food groups, and https://www.acsedu.co.uk/uploads/Food/Lesson%201%20and%20Assignment%201%20Sample%20Human%20Nutrition%20II.pdf.

4 Estimated from Google Maps, for example a walking trip from Cairo to Singapore takes 2290 hrs non-stop (a year has 8760 hours).

5 See https://en.wikipedia.org/wiki/Estimates_of_historical_world_population, which summarises the key studies that estimate population size between 10,000 BC and 3000 BC.

6 Richard H. Wilkinson *The Complete Gods and Goddesses of Ancient Egypt* (Thames and Hudson Ltd, May 2003).

7 https://www.ancient.eu/Utu-Shamash (Joshua J. Mark, 31 January 2017).

8 https://www.thoughtco.com/ancient-maya-astronomy-2136314 (Dr. Christopher Minster, 24 July 2019). I have applied some liberty in attributing later Maya beliefs to the early development of the

civilisation, however, few records exist of that early time, and I feel it is a fair assumption to make, at least to illustrate the point made.

9   https://www.universetoday.com/22570/venus-the-morning-star/.

10   Littleton, C. Scott *Gods, Goddesses, and Mythology* (Benchmark Books; New, 2005).

11   https://blog.britishmuseum.org/solar-eclipses-then-and-now/ (Jonathan Taylor, Curator, Middle East, 21 August 2017).

12   Kevin Leloux "The Battle of the Eclipse (May 28, 585 BC): a discussion of the Lydo-Median treaty and the Halys border" *Polemos* (December 2016) Vol 19-2, 31-54. Available here: https://www.academia.edu/32406140/The_Battle_Of_The_Eclipse _May_28_585_BC_A_Discussion_Of_The_Lydo_Median_Treaty _And_The_Halys_Border_Polemos_19_2_2016_p_31_54.

13   https://penelope.uchicago.edu/Thayer/E/Gazetteer/Topics/astr-onomy/_Texts/secondary/journals/The_Observatory/Eclipse_of_Pe ricles*.html.

14   Dicks, D. R *Early Greek astronomy to Aristotle* (Ithaca, N.Y.: Cornell University Press, 1970).

15   Henry C King *The History of the Telescope* (Dover Publications, 01 September 2003).

16   Jerome J. Langford *Galileo, Science, and the Church* (University of Michigan Press, 31 October 1992).

17   https://science.nasa.gov/science-news/science-at-nasa/2014/23j-ul_superstorm.

All websites noted here reference their version on 02 March 2021 (accessible via https://archive.org/web/, should they have changed since).

About the author

John Almeryn was born in London. He studied Engineering at Christ's College, Cambridge University, before becoming a Chartered Engineer. Later in his career, he qualified as a Patent Attorney. He lives in Derby.

Printed in Great Britain
by Amazon

11871522R00061